MODERN NOVELISTS

General Editor: Norman Page

MODERN NOVELISTS

Published titles

ALBERT CAMUS Philip Thody
FYODOR DOSTOEVSKY Peter Conradi
WILLIAM FAULKNER David Dowling
GUSTAVE FLAUBERT David Roe
E. M. FORSTER Norman Page
WILLIAM GOLDING James Gindin
GRAHAM GREENE Neil McEwan
HENRY JAMES Alan Bellringer
D. H. LAWRENCE G. M. Hyde
DORIS LESSING Ruth Whittaker
MALCOLM LOWRY Tony Bareham
MARCEL PROUST Philip Thody
BARBARA PYM Michael Cotsell
SIX WOMEN NOVELISTS Merryn Williams
MURIEL SPARK Norman Page
JOHN UPDIKE Judie Newman
EVELYN WAUGH Jacqueline McDonnell
H. G. WELLS Michael Draper
VIRGINIA WOOLF Edward Bishop

Forthcoming titles

MARGARET ATWOOD Coral Ann Howells
SAUL BELLOW Paul Hyland
IVY COMPTON-BURNETT Janet Godden
JOSEPH CONRAD Owen Knowles
GEORGE ELIOT Alan Bellringer
F. SCOTT FITZGERALD John Whitley
JOHN FOWLES James Acheson
ERNEST HEMINGWAY Peter Messent
CHRISTOPHER ISHERWOOD Stephen Wade
JAMES JOYCE Richard Brown
NORMAN MAILER Michael Glenday
THOMAS MANN Martin Travers
V. S. NAIPAUL Bruce King
GEORGE ORWELL Valerie Meyers
ANTHONY POWELL Neil McEwan
PAUL SCOTT G. K. Das
PATRICK WHITE Mark Williams

MODERN NOVELISTS

VIRGINIA WOOLF

Edward Bishop

St. Martin's Press   **New York**

First published in the United States of America in 1991

Printed in Hong Kong

ISBN 0–312–04090–3

Library of Congress Cataloging-in-Publication Data
Bishop, Edward.
  Virginia Woolf / Edward Bishop.
    p.   cm. — (Modern novelists)
  Includes bibliographical references and index.
  ISBN 0–312–04090–3
  1. Woolf, Virginia, 1882–1941—Criticism and interpretation.
  I. Title. II. Series.
  PR6045.072Z555   1991
  823′.912—dc20   90–40587
                                                      CIP

Contents

Acknowledgements

I wish to thank Professor Quentin Bell, the British Library, and the Henry W. and Albert A. Berg Collection, New York Public Library, Astor, Lenox and Tilden Foundations for permission to quote from Virginia Woolf's manuscripts.

The Social Sciences and Humanities Research Council of Canada I thank for the grants that enabled me to consult the manuscripts. I want to thank Norman Page for his guidance; my 1989 graduate class for their suggestions; and Foy, Killam and Glancy for their generous advice.

Harold F. Mosher, Jr, for 'Metaphor and the Subversive Process of Virginia Woolf's Essays', reprinted from *Style*, vol. 21, no. 4 (Winter 1987).

Twentieth Century Literature, Hofstra University, for 'The Shaping of *Jacob's Room*', reprinted from this journal, vol. 32 no. 1 (Spring 1986), and for '*The Voyage Out*', reprinted from vol. 27, no. 4 (Winter 1981).

The Fellows and President of Newberry College for 'Pursuing "It" through "Kew Gardens"', reprinted from *Studies in Short Fiction*, vol. 19, no. 3 (Summer 1982).

Every effort has been made to trace all copyright holders, but if any have been inadvertently overlooked the publishers will be pleased to make the necessary arrangement at the first opportunity.

General Editor's Preface

The death of the novel has often been announced, and part of the secret of its obstinate vitality must be its capacity for growth, adaptation, self-renewal and self-transformation: like some vigorous organism in a speeded-up Darwinian ecosystem, it adapts itself quickly to a changing world. War and revolution, economic crisis and social change, radically new ideologies such as Marxism and Freudianism, have made this century unprecedented in human history in the speed and extent of change, but the novel has shown an extraordinary capacity to find new forms and techniques and to accommodate new ideas and conceptions of human nature and human experience, and even to take up new positions on the nature of fiction itself.

In the generations immediately preceding and following 1914, the novel underwent a radical redefinition of its nature and possibilities. The present series of monographs is devoted to the novelists who created the modern novel and to those who, in their turn, either continued and extended, or reacted against and rejected, the traditions established during that period of intense exploration and experiment. It includes a number of those who lived and wrote in the nineteenth century but whose innovative contribution to the art of fiction makes it impossible to ignore them in any account of the origins of the modern novel; it also includes the so-called 'modernists' and those who in the mid- and late twentieth century have emerged as outstanding practitioners of this genre. The scope is, inevitably, international; not only, in the migratory and exile-haunted world of our century, do writers refuse to heed national frontiers – 'English' literature lays claim to Conrad the Pole, Henry James the American, and Joyce the Irishman – but geniuses such as Flaubert, Dostoevsky and Kafka have had an influence on the fiction of many nations.

1
The Writer's Life

And now with some pleasure I find that its seven; & must cook dinner. Haddock & sausage meat. I think it is true that one gains a certain hold on sausage & haddock by writing them down.

(D v, 358)

The tone is whimsical, but the theme most serious. Incendiary bombs were dropping along the Sussex downs, spare petrol was stored in the garage so that she and Leonard could commit suicide in the event of a German invasion, and Virginia herself was struggling to find a meaning in a world where literature itself had become pointless. For Virginia Woolf writing gave a hold not just on sausage and haddock but on life itself.

Writing dominated Woolf's life from the moment of her birth on 25 January 1882. Her father Leslie Stephen was already an eminent Victorian man of letters and in the year of her birth he took on the editorship of the *Dictionary of National Biography*, a project that became part of the rhythm of the lives of the young Stephen children, who could hear the thump of his books on the library floor as he worked. But before Virginia was ten she had begun her own editorial project: publication of the *Hyde Park Gate News*, a weekly newspaper that continued for four years. Her formal education was confined to a few courses at King's College, London, and she would for the rest of her life resent the fact that her brothers, Thoby and Adrian, were sent to Cambridge while she and her sister Vanessa were denied university (an issue that roused her to eloquence in *A Room of One's Own* and *Three Guineas*). The education she valued took place in the private Greek lessons with Janet Case, who fostered an abiding love for the Greek language and Greek literature, and in her father's library, where she was given free rein to read what she liked – and she liked everything.

Though she would become a highly critical reviewer, and though the Greeks, Shakespeare and the Elizabethan prose writers remained her touchstones, until the end of her life she read voraciously in novels, histories and memoirs.

    She spent her summers at St Ives, Cornwall, at Talland House; and the house and the sea would remain central to Woolf's art, figuring not only in the setting of *Jacob's Room* and *To the Lighthouse* but in the rhythm of *The Waves*. Her life was happy, but the death of her mother in 1895, when Virginia was thirteen, brought about her first nervous breakdown; her mother's presence would obsess her until she was in her forties, laid to rest only by the writing of *To the Lighthouse*. Her father was inconsolable, and their London home became a place of unrelenting gloom, with Leslie Stephen making constant demands for sympathy. It was only with her father's death in 1904 that Woolf, at the age of twenty-two, could begin her own life. The Stephen children promptly deserted their home at Hyde Park Gate, Kensington, for deepest Bloomsbury – a district then quite unfashionable. It was in this same year, 1904, that Woolf's first publication appeared, a review in the *Guardian* of W. D. Howells's *The Son of Royal Langbrith* (two months later the young reviewer tackled the new novel by Henry James, *The Golden Bowl*). It is no accident that her father's death and her literary birth coincided. Over twenty years later, in 1928 on the anniversary of his birthday, she writes, 'He would have been ... 96, yes, today; & could have been 96, like other people one has known; but mercifully was not. His life would have entirely ended mine. ... No writing, no books; – inconceivable' (*D* III, 208).

    In 1905, Thoby began holding Thursday evenings at home with his Cambridge friends, Clive Bell, Leonard Woolf, Lytton Strachey and others; this was the beginning of what came to be called the 'Bloomsbury Group'.[1] The group continued and expanded, and figures such as Strachey, Roger Fry and E. M. Forster became lifelong friends. But the next year Woolf's life was shattered by another death: while they were in Greece Thoby contracted typhoid fever and died. This death too would haunt Woolf, and Jacob in *Jacob's Room* and Percival in *The Waves* represent in part her attempt to come to terms with the loss of Thoby. Less obviously, his death figures in *The Voyage Out*, in which the young heroine dies of a tropical fever.

    In 1912, at the age of thirty she married Leonard Woolf. The Woolf marriage has been much analysed, and Leonard cast as both villain and long-suffering martyr, but the letters reveal Virginia's love for him and her need for his admittedly sometimes rigid stability. At this time, they both had finished their first novels, *The Village in the Jungle* and *The Voyage Out*, although Virginia would make extensive revisions to hers. She was anxious about the work, and submitting it to the publishing house of George Duckworth, the half-brother who had sexually molested her, could only have increased her anxiety.[2] She became increasingly unwell, sleeping badly and suffering severe headaches. This went on for months, and eventually, after consulting a specialist, she entered a nursing home. This only made matters worse; the last thing she needed was force-feeding and isolation from those she loved, and she attempted suicide. Publication of *The Voyage Out* was postponed until 1915, and she suffered another breakdown the month before it was published. Depression after finishing a book would become a lifetime pattern, but it was never again so severe until the completion of *Between the Acts*, when it was compounded by the strain of the war.

However, the Woolfs were about to become their own publishers. In 1917 she and Leonard bought a small hand-press and installed it in the dining-room of Hogarth House. They taught themselves to print out of a pamphlet, and two months later produced *Two Stories*, 'The Mark on the Wall' by Virginia and 'Three Jews', by Leonard, with woodcuts by Dora Carrington (the edges of which they cheerfully hacked off with a chisel so the block would not leave lines on the page). It was at about this time that Woolf's friendship with Katherine Mansfield developed. Virginia was shocked by her morals but impressed by her work and her attitude toward art. 'She seems to have gone every sort of hog since she was 17', she wrote to Vanessa, but she 'has a much better idea of writing than most' (*L* II, 159), and in the autumn she began to set the type for Mansfield's story 'Prelude'. Before long they decided they needed a larger press, for Mansfield's story was too big to print one page at a time on the small press, and they took on an assistant, Barbara Hiles. She soon began to irritate them, as all of the many assistants they would have over the years came to do. Leonard liked to retain complete control himself, and tying up parcels was not usually what the young assistants had in mind when they took the job, dreaming of being in the vanguard of literary publishing. Thus although the Hogarth Press was becoming more of an operation it would never become too big, and although they often considered giving it up Virginia retained her share in it until 1938, and Leonard did not sell it until after her death.[3] At this stage, however, the capacity of the Press could be a convenient way of refusing manuscripts.

In April of 1918 Harriet Weaver, who had published James Joyce's *Portrait of the Artist as a Young Man*, came to tea with the manuscript of *Ulysses*. In their polite letter to her a month later they explained that it was too large for the Press. (This was true: Woolf's second novel, *Night and Day*, 1919, conventional in form and far too long for hand-printing, was also published by Duckworth's, and Mansfield's 'Prelude' took eight months from the time they began setting the type until they had finished printing and Virginia had glued, covered and sent out the 300 volumes.) However, Woolf gave her more candid reaction to *Ulysses* in a letter to Lytton Strachey, 'First there's a dog that p's – then there's a man that forths . . . moreover, I don't believe that his method, which is highly developed, means much more than cutting out the explanations and putting in the thoughts between dashes' (*L* II, 234). It would be her new friend T. S. Eliot who would convince her to take the novel more seriously, but she was never enthusiastic about Joyce. Her 'great adventure', as she told Roger Fry four years later as she worked on 'Mrs Dalloway in Bond Street', was Proust: 'the pleasure becomes physical – like sun and wine and grapes and perfect serenity and intense vitality combined. Far otherwise is it with *Ulysses*; to which I bind myself like a martyr to a stake' (*L* II, 565–6).

In the summer of 1919 she and Leonard bought Monk's House in Rodmell, Sussex, which would become their country home for the rest of their lives. Henceforth they would make their twice-yearly migration, down to Rodmell in the spring and back to London at the end of September. At this time she was busy writing reviews (over forty in 1919, for *The Times Literary Supplement* and *Athenaeum*), organising speakers for the Richmond Co-operative Guild, and printing Eliot's *Poems* as well as her own 'Kew Gardens'. These sketches, 'The Mark on the Wall', 'An Unwritten Novel' and 'Kew Gardens', pointed the direction her work would take, and in 1920 she began work on a novel strikingly different from her first two: *Jacob's Room*. Two years later it was finished and after submitting it to Leonard who pronounced it a work of genius (a ritual they would go through with every book except *The Years*), she wrote in her diary with satisfaction, 'There's no doubt in my mind that I have found out how to begin (at 40) to say something in my own voice' (*D* ii, 186). Her long apprenticeship was over.

As always, she was busy with many projects. At the Press they were publishing Dostoevsky's *Stavrogin's Confession*, which she helped translate with their friend S. S. Koteliansky, and works by Andreev, Bunin and Countess Tolstoy. They were also publishing Freud, *Beyond the Pleasure Principle* and *Group Psychology and the Analysis of the Ego* this year (although Woolf maintained she did not read Freud until the 1930s); the Hogarth Press had become the publisher of the official English translations of Freud's works for the International Psycho-Analytical Library. Throughout 1922 she worked with Lady Ottoline Morrell organising a Fellowship Fund to free T. S. Eliot from his job at the bank, continued to read widely for the *Common Reader*, particularly in the Greeks and Chaucer, and found in October of 1922 that 'Mrs Dalloway' was branching into a book. 1922 would be most memorable, however, for the dinner party in December where she met the 'lovely, gifted, aristocratic' Vita Sackville-West. Their friendship developed slowly. In September of 1924 Vita wrote *Seducers in Ecuador* for the Hogarth Press, but it was not until December of 1925 when Virginia spent the weekend at Vita's house that their love affair began. It was a relationship passionate and occasionally sexual but marked by reserves on both sides. Vita admired, was almost intimidated by Virginia's writing; of *To the Lighthouse* she wrote, 'It makes me afraid of you. Afraid of your penetration and loveliness and genius.'[4] Virginia had no such fears of Vita's writing; in fact Vita's patrician airs and her literary aspirations inspired a literary infatuation that issued in *Orlando*, the fantastical biography that begins in 1500 and continues to the present with the hero–heroine changing sex midway through. But Virginia was always jealous of Vita's liaisons with other women and gradually their friendship became more distant. Finally, in March of 1935, after driving down to Sissinghurst (Vita's country house) in a snowstorm, she records the end of the friendship, 'not with a quarrel, not with a bang, but as ripe fruit falls' (*D* iv, 287).

Her only literary friendship was with Katherine Mansfield, and though Woolf was competitive and sometimes snide, anxiously measuring the progress of *Jacob's Room* against the public reaction to *Bliss*, when Mansfield died in January 1923 she felt a great loss: 'Go on writing of course: but into emptiness. There's no competitor' (*D* ii, 229). There was an emptiness of another sort in her life at

this point. In *Mrs Dalloway* Woolf was exploring the 'party consciousness', but more and more, through 1923, she was conscious
of doing it vicariously. Leonard, quite justifiably concerned for her
health, wanted to limit her excitements, but Woolf thrived on
seeing people and she was determined that they must move back
into London – 'I mind missing life far more than he does, for it isn't
life to him in the sense that it is life to me', she wrote in June.– but
Leonard refused. After yet another argument she turned to her
diary, 'baffled & depressed to face a life spent, mute & mitigated, in
the suburbs'. She was writing in the heat of the moment ('I'm
letting my pen fling itself on paper like a leopard starved for
blood') but the passage is revealing of the characters of both
Woolfs, and of the importance of society to Virginia's work:

> This is the pith of my complaint. For ever to be suburban. L. I
> don't think minds any of this as much as I do. But then, Lord!
> (not Lord in K. M. [Katherine Mansfield]'s serious sense) what I
> owe to him! What he gives me! Still, I say, surely we could get
> more from life than we do – isn't he too much of a Puritan, of a
> disciplinarian, doesn't he through birth & training accept a
> drastic discipline too tamely, or rather, with too Spartan a self
> control? There is, I suppose, a very different element in us; my
> social side, his intellectual side. This social side is very genuine in
> me. Nor do I think it reprehensible. It is a piece of jewellery I
> inherit from my mother – a joy in laughter, something that is
> stimulated, not selfishly wholly or vainly, by contact with my
> friends. And then ideas leap in me. Moreover, for my work now,
> I want freer intercourse, wider intercourse – & now, at 41,
> having done a little work, I get my wages partly in invitations. I
> might know people. In Richmond this is impossible.   (*D* ii, 250)

But Virginia finally converted Leonard and in the autumn they
began house-hunting. They returned to the Bloomsbury squares
where Vanessa and many of their friends lived, and in January
moved into 52 Tavistock Square. They were home: although in
1939 they moved to nearby Mecklenburgh Square they never again
moved away from Bloomsbury.

Although taking trains in from Richmond inhibited the spontaneity of London life, Woolf was not really permanently en-
tombed in the suburbs. In April of 1923 they had travelled via Paris
to Granada in Spain, and from there by mule into the Sierra

Nevada to visit Gerald Brenan who was living in the village of Yegen, trying to write. She read Rimbaud and a life of Cézanne, and discussed literature '12 hours every day' with Brenan. Woolf had always been an enthusiastic traveller, and although before the trip to Spain she had not been to the continent for ten years, now that Vanessa spent her winters at Cassis in the south of France she and Leonard would often make that an excuse for a spring trip to Europe.

The trips were made possible, in part, by the commercial success of her novels. At the end of 1924, as she was retyping *Mrs Dalloway* and finishing *The Common Reader* she was already thinking of a story, 'The Old Man', that would evolve into *To the Lighthouse*. This book she would write more quickly and more easily than any of her works to date. Early in 1927, ten days before her forty-fifth birthday (25 January), she finished the typescript. It was well received, and it bought her and Leonard their first motor-car. 'I can think of nothing else', she wrote to Ethel Sands, 'I have driven from the Embankment to Marble Arch and only knocked one boy very gently off his bicycle. But I would rather have a gift for motoring than anything' (*L* III, 400). She in fact didn't have the gift and eventually abandoned driving lessons, but it was her growing financial independence that was important to her:

> All this money making originated in a spasm of black despair one night at Rodmell [15 Sept. 1926]. . . . (part of my misery was the perpetual limitation of everything; no chairs, or beds, no comfort, no beauty; & no freedom to move: all of which I determined there & then to win). And so came to an agreement with Leonard about sharing money after a certain sum; & then opened a bank account. . . . The important thing is to spend freely, without fuss or anxiety. (*D* III, 212; see also 112, 164, 175)

Orlando, published the next year, brought even greater sales (though initially it did poorly because booksellers insisted upon shelving it under 'Biography') and increased fame (including tea at Lady Cunard's) but Woolf recognised that though she had learned continuity, narrative and how to write a direct sentence from *Orlando*, she had not explored as she had in *To the Lighthouse*. And there had been something she had known for some time that she would want to move into: the mystical side of her dark moods. In

1926 she had written, 'It is not oneself but something in the universe that one's left with. . . . One sees a fin passing far out', striking the image that would lie at the heart of *The Waves* (*D* III, 113). Two years later she was slowly starting to work on the novel, holding herself back until she could 'saturate every atom', get away from 'this appalling narrative business of the realist' (*D* III, 209). Meanwhile she was struggling with her work of criticism, 'Phases of Fiction', and writing up the two lectures on 'Women and Fiction' that she had delivered at Cambridge in October. These lectures became *A Room of One's Own*, a work now central to modern feminism, in which she explores many issues connected with women and writing but above all insists on the irrevocable link between economic independence and artistic independence: thus the need for a woman to have £500 a year and 'a room of one's own' if she is to write.

In 1929 she began to work on *The Waves* in earnest, but it went slowly. As the manuscript reveals, Woolf toiled through two complete and very different drafts before achieving the published form of the text. There was nothing like the fluency of *To the Lighthouse* this time; she found herself writing and rewriting until her manuscript book was like a 'lunatic's dream' (*D* III, 275). The reference to lunacy is not fortuitous. With this book Woolf seemed to be drawing on the deepest sources of her creative energy, and she recognised that there was some obscure connection between her creative processes and her illnesses, both physical and mental. In bed with one of the bouts of influenza that plagued her all her life, she writes, 'Once or twice I have felt that odd whirr of wings in the head which comes when I am ill so often. . . . If I could stay in bed another fortnight (but there is no chance of that) I believe I should see the whole of The Waves' (*D* III, 286). When she did finish the book it was in a creative burst that seemed close to madness:

> I wrote the words O Death fifteen minutes ago, having reeled across the last ten pages with some moments of such intensity & intoxication that I seemed only to stumble after my own voice, or almost, after some sort of speaker (as when I was mad). . . . I have netted that fin in the waste of waters . . . (*D* IV, 10)

The exultation succeeded to the usual depression after finishing a book, and she was saddened as well by the death of her old rival,

Arnold Bennett, who in spite of his 'shopkeepers view of literature' had, she felt, some 'real understanding power', and she 'rather wished him to go on abusing me; & me abusing him' (*D* IV, 16). Woolf was always more generous with her contemporaries once they were dead. On their trip to western France in the spring of 1931 she read D. H. Lawrence's *Sons and Lovers* and *The Man Who Died*, realising with regret that a 'man of genius' had written in her time and she had never read him (he had died the year before). She noted that they had much in common, but 'its the preaching that rasps me' and, as with Joyce, compared him unfavourably to Proust, the only contemporary for whom she had ever expressed unqualified admiration (*D* IV, 25, 29, 126). 'The fact about contemporaries', she wrote to Ethel Smyth from La Rochelle, 'is that they're doing the same thing on another railway line: one resents their distracting one, flashing past, the wrong way'; and in fact the only time she saw Lawrence was briefly, from a train in Palermo, Sicily, before his train and hers parted in opposite directions (*L* IV, 315; III, 361).

Katherine Mansfield still haunted her and in early June Woolf dreamed of meeting her beyond death. The deaths would come more frequently in the 1930s – Roger Fry (1934), Janet Case (1937), Ottoline Morrell (1939) – but the first to go of the friends she had grown up with was Lytton Strachey. By the end of 1931 she knew that he had not been avoiding her because he did not like *The Waves*: he had cancer. He died five days before her fiftieth birthday, and Woolf was at first too numbed to do much more than record the event in her diary. Later, as she worked on *Flush*, her biography of Elizabeth Barrett Browning's dog, she felt 'the point is rather gone, as I meant it for a joke with Lytton, and a skit on him' (*L* V, 83). The deaths of close friends always had this effect on her, giving her the feeling that she was writing into a void. It would be this feeling that would finally shake her confidence in her own writing altogether.

On 20 January 1931 a new project had interrupted *The Waves*: out of a speech she was writing for the National Society for Women's Service, she had conceived a sequel to *A Room of One's Own*, to be called 'Professions for Women', and for the next few days could think of nothing else. This was a moment as significant as her vision of the fin in the waste of waters for it was the genesis of the project that would dominate the next five years of her life: *The Pargiters*, the 'Essay-Novel' that would bring her to the edge of madness and would eventually split into two books, *The Years* (1937) and *Three Guineas* (1938).[5]

Now she was immersed in that work. At the end of 1932 and into 1933 she worked swiftly on *The Pargiters*. She was a success: *Flush* had been chosen as the Book Society's choice of the month, Manchester University had offered her an honorary doctorate (which she declined as she did all such distinctions), royalty cheques had bought her and Leonard a new car which they drove to Italy in May. Their spring trips were becoming more extensive: the previous year they had travelled to Greece, and Virginia vowed to come every year; now after this trip she wanted to buy a house in Italy. She and Leonard often considered, more seriously, buying a house in the south of France near Vanessa, though the idea of managing three homes always finally deterred them.

But there were new forces in Italy to contend with: in October the Hogarth Press published *The Political and Social Doctrine of Fascism* by Benito Mussolini (translated by Jane Soames) and in February of 1934, though she writes excitedly to Quentin Bell that 'I dined with [Lady Sybil] Colefax and met Noel Coward; and he called me Darling. . . . then he played his new opera on Sybils grand piano and sang like a tipsy crow', she strikes a darker note in the next paragraph: 'You are much nearer Vienna [where the Austrian Nazis had staged a *coup d'état*] than I am – but everybody says here this was the beginning of the end. We are to have Mosley [British fascist leader] within five years' (*L* v, 276–7).

In 1934 the Woolfs abandoned the continent in favour of some place more exotic – Ireland. Virginia was fascinated by the conversation of the Irish and wondered in her diary, 'Why arent these people the greatest novelists in the world' (*D* IV, 213). The next spring Leonard and Virginia travelled to Europe again. They crossed over to Holland, drove into Germany, and found themselves surrounded by anti-Jewish banners, in the middle of a reception organised for Goering. They managed to pass through without incident, partly because the soldiers were fascinated by the pet marmoset Leonard carried on his shoulder, but the world had changed. In the coming months Virginia's diary increasingly records political events; one can see them closing in on her. In September 1935 she decided to call her book *The Years*, and noted that that same day the League of Nations was meeting in Geneva to try to find some way of averting the use of force by Mussolini in Abyssinia. In 1936, as Hitler occupied the Rhineland, Woolf struggled with *The Years*, alternating between feeling that it was her best book and that it was an utter failure. She sent the first batch of typescript off to the printers without having Leonard read it beforehand – the first time she had done this, and an index of her unease about the novel. Their conversations revolved endlessly around politics: 'Its odd, how near the guns have got to our private life again ... though I go on, like a doomed mouse, nibbling at my daily page' (*D* v, 17). In April she collapsed and spent most of the month in bed with severe headaches, the growing turmoil in Europe part of the turmoil in her mind.

By July, however, she was working six hours a day, though still racked with doubts about the work, and by November had cut *The Years* from 700 to 420 pages. Nevertheless, the events on the continent were even more unsettling and coming closer to home: Madrid was under bombardment and her nephew Julian Bell was planning to leave his university position in China to fight in the Spanish Civil War. The only topic that supplanted Germany and Spain in the press was Edward VIII's abdication to marry Wallis Simpson.

Through 1937 she worked on *Three Guineas*, the essay complement to *The Years*, which explores discursively what the novel dramatises: the inherent fascism of patriarchy, and the continuum between household tyranny and political tyranny. The book has a directness and an often bitter humour that seldom leaks out in *A Room of One's Own*, and which has challenged and alienated readers. Of all Woolf's works it is the one that is just beginning to be appreciated, rather than simply acclaimed or denounced. In 1937 Woolf also began reading through letters and articles in preparation for what would be her least-read work, the biography of *Roger Fry*. She had been asked to write it and she soon wished she had refused, for she hated the fetters of chronology and fact.

Julian Bell, back from China, was scathing about Roger Fry and all the Bloomsbury intellectuals, and critical of an education which had left him at twenty-nine with only a 'vague literary smattering' (*D* v, 86). In June he left for Spain as an ambulance driver. That summer *The Years* reached the top of the bestseller list in the *New York Herald Tribune* and stayed there for weeks. But it was not a triumph Woolf could enjoy: on 18 July Julian was killed by a shell fragment. Virginia was deeply shaken, both by his death and by the impulse that had driven him to it. In her memoir she remembers how she fixed the details of the farewell dinner party in her mind –

the hot June night, Julian's arguing about politics with Leonard and Clive, his trouble starting the car as he left – because of a sense that he would certainly be killed, and she struggles to understand his determination to go:

> What made him do it? I suppose its a fever in the blood of the younger generation which we can't possibly understand. I have never known anyone of my generation have that feeling about a war. We were all C.O.'s in the Great War. And though I understand that this is a 'cause', can be called the cause of liberty & so on, still my natural reaction is to fight intellectually: if I were any use, I should write against it: I should evolve some plan for fighting English tyranny. The moment force is used it becomes meaningless & unreal to me.   (Bell ɪɪ, 259)

But the violence was only beginning. After finishing *Three Guineas* she immediately began making up 'Pointz Hall', the novel that would become *Between the Acts*. She enjoyed it immensely, as she did all her books at the beginning, and found it a relief from having to shuffle facts for *Roger Fry*. Some facts, however, she could not ignore: Hitler had begun massing troops on the border of Czechoslovakia. He has 'his hounds only very lightly held' she writes in the diary, and the next morning in *Between the Acts* she has Giles think of Europe bristling with guns like a 'hedgehog' (*D* v, 164). In September of 1939 Germany invaded Poland and Britain declared war. Woolf sewed black-out curtains and tried to anchor her mind by reading Greek; she noted in her diary that her own writing still seems more real to her than the war, a conviction she clung to into the closing months of 1940 but which became increasingly difficult to sustain.

In May Germany invaded Holland and Belgium and the Woolfs were now keeping the supply of petrol in the garage so they could asphyxiate themselves when the invasion came. While Virginia continued with *Between the Acts*, small boats criss-crossed the channel evacuating troops from Dunkirk. She pushed on with her memoir, 'A Sketch of the Past', and corrected the proofs of *Roger Fry* but her heart was not in it: 'It struck me that one curious feeling is, that the writing "I", has vanished. No audience. No echo. Thats part of one's death' (*D* v, 293). Later in June, as she read Freud to try to 'centre' herself, she returned to this lack of an echo:

Those familiar circumvolutions – those standards – which have for so many years given back an echo & so thickened my identity are all wide & wild as the desert now. . . . We pour to the edge of a precipice . . . & then? I cant conceive that there will be a 27th June 1941. (*D* v, 299; first ellipsis added)

Through August the Battle of Britain raged, with daily air raids. Vita Sackville-West phoned from Sissinghurst where bombs were dropping around the house; the village next to Rodmell was strafed by fighters. During mid-August, the week of heaviest losses for the Luftwaffe, Ben Nicolson (Vita's son), who had somehow found time to read *Roger Fry* between shifts on an anti-aircraft battery, wrote criticising Fry for living in a fool's paradise. Woolf vigorously defended Roger Fry and Bloomsbury, but art seemed more and more fragile against the bombs, less and less likely to find an audience (*L* vi, 419–22).

She continued to read and to work on *Between the Acts*, but noted that even the weather now was talked about in terms of how it affected a possible invasion or the air raids. She was happy at least that the bombing of the river Ouse had turned the field adjoining Monk's House into an inland sea. In late November she finished *Between the Acts*; she was pleased with it, feeling that it was more 'quintessential' than her other books. Yet as she worked over the typescript she began to doubt again, and by the spring felt it was too slight to be published; and worse than the incendiary bombs along the downs was the fact that there was 'No audience. No private stimulus, only this outer roar' (*L* vi, 479). She found she herself could not read novelists any more.

Finally she could stand it no longer. On March 1941 she wrote to Leonard, 'I feel certain that I am going mad again: I feel we cant go through another of those terrible times. And I shant recover this time. I begin to hear voices and cant concentrate.' She ends, 'I dont think two people could have been happier than we have been' (*L* vi, 481). She then drowned herself in the river Ouse. She was fifty-nine.

Yet the audience she feared the war had obliterated has only grown, and for a generation fascinated by her work the best account of her artistic practice appears in that memoir she was writing in 1940, 'A Sketch of the Past', unpublished until 1976. There she describes how for her life consists predominantly of what she calls 'non-being', a sort of 'nondescript cotton wool', in which are embedded moments of heightened consciousness during which one is in contact with the reality that underlies everyday life: 'moments of being' –:

> Every day includes much more non-being than being. Yesterday for example, Tuesday the 18th of April, was [as] it happened a good day; above the average in 'being'. It was fine; I enjoyed writing these first pages; my head was relieved of the pressure of writing about Roger; I walked over Mount Misery and along the river. . . . I also read Chaucer with pleasure; and began a book – the memoirs of Madame de la Fayette – which interested me. These separate moments of being were however embedded in many more moments of non-being.   (p. 70)

Significantly, the experience becomes 'real' and 'whole', where before it was inchoate, only when she puts it into words. When she was young, she writes, the 'shock' of reality was just a 'sledge-hammer blow' that often brought with it 'a peculiar horror and a physical collapse'. Not until she was older did she discover that the shock could have a positive effect:

> It is not, as I thought as a child, simply a blow from the enemy hidden behind the cotton wool of daily life; it is or will become a revelation of some order; it is a token of some real thing behind appearances and I make it real by putting it into words. It is only by putting it into words that I make it whole.   (p. 72)

Words for Woolf do not simply translate a given perception into a conceptual form: they serve to bring fully into being, and to sustain, the perception. Her shock discloses its import only through the process of 'making whole'. She notes that the perception 'is so instinctive that it seems given to me, not made by me' (p. 72); and in a later passage she emphasises that the realising through language also takes place instinctively:

> These scenes, by the way, are not altogether a literary device – a means of summing up and making innumerable details visible in one concrete picture. . . . I find that scene making is my natural

way of marking the past. Always a scene has arranged itself: representative; enduring.... Is this liability to scenes the origin of my writing impulse?   (p. 122)

The workings of her creative process become visible here: aside from the conscious 'summing up' she simultaneously 'makes' and is 'liable to' scenes. That is, she does not so much construct as assist the self-declarative arrangement of the scene. When she explains the significance of these moments she does so figuratively; she confirms that the experience has value but hesitates to assign meaning. It gives her, she says,

> a great delight to put the severed parts together. Perhaps this is the strongest pleasure known to me. It is the rapture I get in writing when I seem to be discovering what belongs to what. ... From this I reach what I might call a philosophy; at any rate it is a constant idea of mine; that behind the cotton wool is hidden a pattern; that we – I mean all human beings – are connected with this; that we are parts of the work of art. ... And this I see when I have a shock.   (p. 72)

Later in the essay, in her discussion of 'scene making', Woolf returns to her theory of a reality intermittently glimpsed, and she denies any attempt to approach it rationally:

> This confirms me in my instinctive notion: (it will not bear arguing about; it is irrational) the sensation that we are sealed vessels afloat on what it is convenient to call reality; and at some moments, the sealing matter cracks; in floods reality; that is, these scenes.   (p. 122)

Her analogies – the world as a work of art, individuals as sealed vessels – although hardly novel do satisfy us. Yet if we pause we find them contradictory, confusing. The scenes, for example, seem to be constellations of details, then in the next breath they are described in a manner more appropriate to undifferentiated sensation. One can go a long way toward reconciling these disparities, but her figures resist such efforts. In both her fiction and her discursive prose they remain deliberately irrational and untranslatable. She employs them here as she does in *The Waves*, 'never making them work out; only suggest' (*D* IV, 11). The 'revelation of order' takes precedence over the 'concrete picture'.

She brings the role of language and the reader more sharply into focus when she recalls the sensation of suddenly understanding a familiar poem for the first time, an experience akin to her process of composition:

> It was as if it became altogether intelligible; I had a feeling of transparency in words when they cease to be words and become so intensified that one seems to experience them; to foretell them as if they developed what one is already feeling.... It matches what I have sometimes felt when I write. The pen gets on the scent.   (p. 93)

Ideally, the process of reading, like that of 'making whole', renders intelligible without logically explaining. The insight she records is non-rational, and something one is given and at the same time intuitively fashions. The abstraction of words dissolves and they impinge upon the senses, at once foretold and actively developing the reader's thoughts. The work of art, then, must do more than describe; it must lead the reader to the point where he or she can apprehend the writer's vision. This becomes Woolf's major artistic concern: how to create this heightened awareness in the reader. Even when she presents her 'philosophy' she is less concerned to impart information or argue a position than she is to initiate a process.

From the beginning of her career she grappled with questions of language. As a theoretical concern it pervades her essays, letters and diary, and it bulks large in her fiction as well. In fact, nearly all Woolf's major characters, from Rachel in *The Voyage Out* to Miss La Trobe in *Between the Acts*, are concerned with the elusive role of language in ordering reality, in apprehending others, in constituting the self. And as the title of the next chapter suggests, Woolf's art was from the first always taking risks, pushing beyond the safe limits of discourse, arcing toward the far side of language.

2

The Voyage Out: Towards the Far Side of Language

One of Virginia Woolf's most eloquent statements on the role of language appears in her essay 'On Not Knowing Greek' where she asserts that, in order to understand Aeschylus,

> it is not so necessary to understand Greek as to understand poetry. It is necessary to take that dangerous leap through the air without the support of words which Shakespeare also asks of us. . . . Connecting them in a rapid flight of the mind we know instantly and instinctively what they mean, but could not decant that meaning afresh into other words. The meaning is just on the far side of language.   (C I, 7)

The passage accurately describes the workings of Woolf's own mature art, yet even in her first novel, *The Voyage Out* (1915), language attains the concentration and suggestiveness of poetry. The novel rewards patient analysis, for in Rachels' restive questioning of the functions of language, Woolf introduces what will become a persistent theme in all her works: the problem of how words can encompass and communicate human experience. Further, it is in *The Voyage Out* that one discovers Woolf labouring to achieve what she would later effect with felicitous ease: a mode of discourse which compels the reader's active participation, guiding us to the point where we can make our own intuitive leap, to apprehend a reality that will not submit to denotative prose.

It was not until the spring of 1919, with the publication of 'Modern Fiction' and 'Kew Gardens' (manifestos in complementary modes), that she publicly announced her artistic intentions. However, in a letter to Clive Bell written in 1908 as she was

17

beginning to shape 'Melymbrosia', later *The Voyage Out*, she declared:

> I think a great deal of my future, and settle what book I am to write – how I shall re-form the novel and capture multitudes of things at present fugitive, enclose the whole, and shape infinite strange shapes. I take a good look at woods in the sunset, and fix men who are breaking stones with an intense gaze, meant to sever them from the past and the future – all these excitements last out my walk, but tomorrow I know, I shall be sitting down to the inanimate old phrases. (*L* I, 356)

The young woman's bold plans to reform promise to lead her away from traditional concepts of plot and character, for her interest lies less in the variables of personality than in the radical character of human beings and things, both animate and inanimate, of the external world; she wants to 'sever them from past and future', and she intends not merely to record but to 'capture' and 'shape' this elusive aspect of reality. But her enthusiasm for rejuvenating fiction is suddenly punctured by the thought of contending with the 'inanimate old phrases'. One notices throughout Woolf's writings a constantly fluctuating regard for language: it strikes her by turns as an almost magical force, as a mere necessary evil, and as a betrayer of life. These disparate attitudes inform *The Voyage Out*, and the work is both a groping exploration on Woolf's part of the connection between reality and language, and a dramatic portrayal of a corresponding exploration in the growth of the central character.

The novel traces Rachel Vinrace's voyage out: a journey from England to South America, an initiation in to love, and finally a passage out of life into death. In a concurrent mental voyage that leads both inward and outward, Rachel awakens to the world at large and to her own consciousness. She discovers that life can seem very precarious and the world entirely desolate, only to decide later that the world is a most hospitable place and life something calm and certain. She finds it difficult to put either perception into words, and the problem arises as much from the uncertain nature of reality as it does from language. As it does for characters in Woolf's subsequent novels, Rachel's progress takes shape around 'moments of being', instants of almost visionary insight in which her understanding of life is sharply, and somewhat disconcertingly, enhanced.

After their arrival in South America, Rachel's companion, the older and more worldly Helen Ambrose, desires 'that Rachel should think, and for this reason offered books' (p. 123). Helen's prescription proves to be well-advised. The reading does make Rachel think – and in a manner that contrasts sharply both with the packrat-like cataloguing of her fellow tourist, Mr Pepper, and with the pedantry of Helen's husband, Ridley Ambrose. The books engender a curiosity about life itself: 'What is the truth? What is the truth of it all?' she asks, Her new curiosity about 'the truth of it all' derives as much from that sense of 'wonder which always marks the transition from the imaginary world to the real world' (p. 122), as it does from the specific contents of the books. After reading she finds that 'the landscape outside . . . now appeared amazingly solid and clear' (p. 122). The sensation of gazing upon or seeing the world, rather than merely looking at it, leaves Rachel ripe for the visionary experience that translates her disinterested curiosity into a vital personal concern. Here the side effects of reading act as the catalyst for a more intense and more disturbing apprehension of the phenomenal world:

> The morning was hot, and the exercise of reading left her mind contracting and expanding like the mainspring of a clock. . . . Her dissolution became so complete that she could not raise her finger any more, and sat perfectly still, listening and looking always at the same spot. It became stranger and stranger. She was overcome with awe that things should exist at all. . . . She forgot that she had any fingers to raise. . . . She continued to be conscious of these vast masses of substance for a long stretch of time, the clock still ticking in the midst of the universal silence.   (p. 124; first ellipsis added)

Reading involves cognition that is both rational and perceptual, and whether or not Woolf had this in mind when she spoke of the 'contracting and expanding' of Rachel's mind, it is the *act* of reading rather than the meaning of the words that triggers Rachel's experience. Now at the furthest possible remove from intellection, her question, 'What is the truth of it all?' becomes something felt rather than entertained, replaced by a fundamental 'awe that things should exist at all'. This awe constitutes only the preliminary stage of Rachel's awakening, however, for she has perceived existence only, not the life of things nor the relations between them.

Immediately following her bleak vision, an invitation to a picnic affects her with unusual force: 'The blood began to run in her veins; she felt her eyes brighten. "We must go," she said, rather surprising Helen by her decision. "We must certainly go" – such was the relief of finding that things still happened, and indeed they appeared the brighter for the mist surrounding them' (p. 125). The 'things that happen' are the bonds between human beings. Terence Hewet, who sent the note, underlines its significance: '"Cows" he reflected, "draw together in a field; ships in a calm; and we're just the same when we've nothing else to do. But why do we do it – is it just to prevent ourselves from seeing to the bottom of things ... or do we really love each other ...?"' (p. 126). It is communion, with others and with the external world, that separates the process of life from the stasis of pure existence. Rachel has begun to feel the necessity of love in its broadest sense.

Woolf extends the word 'love' to include the complete and intimate knowing of anything outside the self. And human love is often (though not necessarily) a precursor to this larger sympathy, engaging the intuitive mode of perception through which one on rare occasions becomes immersed in the reality beneath the surfaces of life. Rachel's second brush with pure existence, which occurs after she has begun to fall in love, brings with it a sense of meaning. Filled with an 'unreasonable exultation', she wanders aimlessly into the hills:

> So she might have walked until she had lost all knowledge of her way, had it not been for the interruption of a tree, which, although it did not grow across her path, stopped her as effectively as if the branches had struck her in the face. It was an ordinary tree, but to her it appeared so strange that it might have been the only tree in the world. ... Having seen a sight that would last her for a lifetime, and for a lifetime would preserve that second, the tree once more sank into the ordinary ranks of trees, and she was able to seat herself in its shade. (p. 174).

At a dance the previous evening Rachel had declared, '"I've changed my view of life completely"' (p. 162); and though Helen had scoffed, the occasion does mark the beginning of a new perception in Rachel. For Woolf, affinities exist not only among people but among all things (a notion she will develop more extensively in *Mrs Dalloway*), and to experience this web of relation is to be immersed in what she calls reality. This is precisely what was missing in Rachel's first vision. It brought her to an awareness of existence only, where her second granted her an apprehension of reality.

The communion with what lies outside the self occupies a central place in all Woolf's novels, and Rachel herself later analyses the relation between human love and the empathy that one may establish with things. When Terence, irked with her ability to 'cut herself adrift from him, and to pass away to unknown places where she had no need of him', charges her with 'always wanting something else', she admits to herself that 'what he was saying was perfectly true, and that she wanted many more things than the love of one human being – the sea, the sky' (p. 309). In this she anticipates Woolf's later protagonists, most of whom feel the attraction of the nonhuman realm. Upon entering Greece Jacob Flanders discovers 'how tremendously pleasant it is to be alone. . . . to have – positively – a rush of friendship for stones and grasses, as if humanity were over' (*JR*, 137). Peter Walsh feels the same lure in his dreams of the solitary traveller, the 'desire for solace, for relief, for something outside these . . . craven men and women' (*MD*, 52). That 'solace' tempts Mrs Ramsay at the beginning of the dinner when she wishes to avoid the effort of creating, to find instead 'rest on the floor of the sea', and Lily watches her 'drifting into that strange no-man's land' (*TL*, 79). But just as Mrs Ramsay gives herself a shake and turns to Bankes, so Rachel eventually, reluctantly, acknowledges that she cannot dispense with this imperfect and mutable world, and that the capacity for human love and the ability to penetrate what she calls the 'curtain' of external reality are somehow linked.

Near the close of the book she slips into a reverie that counterpoints her first vision of desolation. Life, which had seemed to be 'only a light passing over the surface and vanishing' (p. 124), now through the agency of love has taken on a meaningful pattern:

one thing led to another and by degrees something had formed itself out of nothing, and so one reached at last this calm, this quiet, this certainty, and it was this process that people called living. . . . Why should this insight ever again desert her? The world was in truth so large, so hospitable, and after all it was so simple. 'Love,' St John had said, 'that seems to explain it all.' Yes, but it was not the love of man for woman, of Terence for

Rachel. . . . they had ceased to struggle and desire one another.
There seemed to be peace between them. It might be love, but it
was not the love of man for woman.   (pp. 321–2)

She argues to herself that the 'love of man for woman' is relatively
unimportant in reaching 'this calm, this quiet, this certainty' in life's
harmony. But, she finally concedes, maybe one cannot renounce it
after all:

> although she was going to marry him and to live with him for
> thirty, or forty, or fifty years, and to quarrel, and to be so close to
> him; she was independent of him; she was independent of
> everything else. Nevertheless, as St John said, it was love that
> made her understand this, for she had never felt this independ-
> ence, this calm, and this certainty until she fell in love with him,
> and perhaps this too was love.   (p. 322)

She had begun to acquire the understanding that is Woolf's
measure of true maturity: the knowledge that what seem to be
polar opposites are most often complementary aspects of the same
reality – that, as James Ramsay discovers of the lighthouse,
'nothing was simply one thing' (*TL*, 286).
   The same paradoxical complexity proves characteristic of language as well, and Woolf explores the problem dramatically,
incorporating it in the growth of Rachel's love for Terence. Just
after her encounter with the tree, Rachel discovers that 'the very
words of books were steeped in radiance' (p. 175). As she reads a
passage in Gibbon even the unexotic words become intensified:

> Never had any words been so vivid and so beautiful – Arabia
> Felix – Aethiopia. But those were not more noble than the
> others, hardy barbarians, forests, and morasses. They seemed to
> drive roads back to the very beginning of the world, on either
> side of which the populations of all times and countries stood in
> avenues, and by passing down them all knowledge would be
> hers, and the book of the world turned back to the very first
> page.   (p. 175)

Before this time she had read 'with the curious literalness of one to
whom written sentences are unfamiliar, and handling words as
though they were made of wood, separately of great importance,

and possessed of shapes like tables or chairs' (p. 123). Now for the
first time she has apprehended the essence of words: not just the
import of Gibbon's prose, but of language itself.[1] Although at first
glance it appears as if the events have little in common, other than a
shared origin in her new love, the juxtaposition highlights their
similarity.

At the close of her walk through the countryside, after reading
Gibbon, Rachel seeks the origins of the 'exultation' which precipi-
tated her visionary experience. She narrows the possible causes to
Terence and his friend, St John Hirst:

> Any clear analysis of them was impossible owing to the haze of
> wonder in which they were enveloped.... She then became
> haunted by a suspicion which she was so reluctant to face that she
> welcomed a trip and stumble over the grass.... 'What is it to be
> in love?' she demanded, after a long silence; each word as it came
> into being seemed to shove itself out into an unknown
> sea. (pp. 175–6)

Rachel emerges from her confusion as her emotions force themselves into language, almost against her will. As the metaphor
suggests, to use language is to launch oneself on a voyage out, for
once formulated the question reveals new implications: she is 'awed
by the discovery of a terrible possibility in life' (p. 176). Woolf chose
to emphasise this, for in *Melymbrosia* the episode is merely the flush
of infatuation. Rachel's question is 'Am I in love?', rather than the
more reflective, 'What is it to be in love?', and the words of Gibbon
do not 'drive roads back to the very beginning of the world' and
generate 'excitement at the possibilities of knowledge now opening
before her', they are simply part of a general euphoria:

> It was the fullness of the life in everything. What words those
> were on the opposite page – Aethiopia – Arabia Felix! Even the
> leaves, and the hills seemed to have a tremendous motion in
> them.[2]

In the published text Rachel's discovery is more profound, as she
learns that articulation may be heuristic as well as declarative.

Yet later on, after she and Terence have become engaged, the
word 'love' frustrates precise definition of her feelings. Vexed with
the platitudes of congratulation, she snaps, 'I never fell in love, if

falling in love is what people say it is, and it's the world that tells the lies and I tell the truth' (p. 300). But communicating this truth proves not to be a simple matter. In her replies 'she produced phrases which bore a considerable likeness to those which she had condemned. She was struck by it herself, for she stopped writing and looked up . . . and was amazed at the gulf which lay between all that and her sheet of paper. Would there ever be a time when the world was one and indivisible?' (pp. 302–3). In fact, when reading Gibbon she had transcended the gulf between words and external reality; for a moment the world had seemed to be one and indivisible. However, such identity does not remain long intact, and if the word captures experience, yet in fixing and defining it also limits. Although the word begins by presenting immediate sensory experience to the intellect, it evolves into a cipher, losing the original sensory imprint as it becomes a vehicle for abstract thought. Language begins to constrict and distort that same experience which it brought to light.

One difficulty derives from the fact that emotions cannot be grasped by the lapel; as Woolf pointedly demonstrates, insight into the emotional state of oneself or another can best be achieved indirectly. Upon leaving Rachel after they have declared their love, Terence indulges in the rehearsal of their conversation that lovers can never resist and inevitably find excruciating:

> He ran his mind over the things they had said, the random, unnecessary things which had eddied round and round and used up all the time, and drawn them so close together and flung them so far apart, and left him in the end unsatisfied, ignorant still of what she felt and of what she was like. What was the use of talking, talking, merely talking?   (p. 224)

Yet they have gained in intimacy. In later works Woolf will more emphatically affirm the generative value of 'merely talking': Clarissa Dalloway feels that her parties are 'an offering; to combine, to create', which provide the opportunity for individuals to 'go much deeper' and thereby connect with 'this thing she called life' (*MD*, 109); and at the outset of her dinner, Mrs Ramsay deliberately resorts to her 'social' language as the first step in weaving the group into harmony around the Boeuf en Daube (*TL*, 84). The semantic content may be minimal, but such exchanges create a tone, a mood, and in fact for Terence and Rachel the 'random unnecessary things' prove far more effective than the formal biographical sketches that Hirst had demanded during an earlier meeting. They feel 'more intimate because they shared the knowledge of what eight o'clock in Richmond meant' (p. 223); and their discussion brings them to the point where they can make the leap of understanding implicit in the highly charged though outwardly prosaic exchange,

> 'I like you: d'you like me?' Rachel suddenly observed.
> 'I like you immensely,' Hewet replied.   (p. 223)

The words here lose their colloquial vacuity and carry an emotional charge disproportionate to their denotative meaning. They do so precisely because neither party tries to fix the emotion, allowing the words instead to orient the flow of understanding which takes place finally beyond language.

The ideal would be somehow to capture and communicate experience without reducing it to 'inanimate phrases'. This quintessential communication is what Terence (who speaks here for Woolf) hopes to achieve through art. He intends to convey the inner life, to present those things that cannot be baldly stated: his novel will be 'about Silence ... the things people don't say', although his smugness might cause us to doubt his fitness for such a delicate task – 'I'm good second rate; about as good as Thackeray' (pp. 220–1). Yet literature can be a means of grasping the reality normally veiled both in human relations and in the external world. Echoing Woolf's letter in which she speaks of severing character from past and future, Terence asserts that the advantage of his projected 'Stuart tragedy' is that 'detached from modern conditions, one can make [characters] more intense and more abstract then people who live as we do' (p. 222). And of writing in general he observes:

> What I want to do in writing novels is very much what you want to do when you play the piano, I expect,' he began, turning and speaking over his shoulder. 'We want to find out what's behind things, don't we? – Look at the lights down there,' he continued, 'scattered about anyhow.... Have you ever seen fireworks that makes figures? ... I want to make figures.'   (pp. 223–4; Woolf's ellipses)

In spite of his *naïveté*, in this image Terence expresses the discovery, ordering and incandescent communication that takes place in the execution of a fully realised work of art.[3]

Terence does not doubt the worth of his enterprise, although he concedes that it will not be easy:

> 'The difficulty is immense.... And yet I sometimes wonder whether there's anything else in the whole world worth doing. These other people,' he indicated the hotel, 'are always wanting something they can't get. But there's an extraordinary satisfaction in writing, even in the attempt to write. What you said just now is true: one doesn't want to be things; one wants merely to be allowed to see them.' (p. 220)

This conviction of the value of art, for oneself and for the human race, remains constant in Woolf's writings. In 'The Patron and the Crocus', written in 1925, she develops the thesis that a writer and his or her readers are bound 'by more than material tie': 'the crocus is an imperfect crocus until it has been shared' (*CE* II, 149–50). And in 'A Sketch of the Past' (1940) she echoes Terence's concern for the pattern behind things, and expresses with even greater force her belief in the importance of writing in creating and sustaining civilisation:

> [My conception] is that there is a pattern hid behind the cotton wool. And this conception affects me every day. I prove this, now, by spending the morning writing, when I might be walking, running a shop, or learning to do something that will be useful if war comes. I feel that by writing I am doing what is far more necessary than anything else. (*MB*, 73)

These three statements, spanning a quarter of a century, point to the work of art not as a means of resolving a personal need (although it is certainly that as well), but as something that creates communion: both by affording others a glimpse of the pattern of which we are all a part, and by expressing those things which we may sense but cannot express – 'the things people don't say' and which, without the artist's guidance, we cannot articulate at all.

Yet Terence will not be the one to do it. He is threatened by Rachel's love for 'the sea, the sky' (p. 309); this love, however, is the love of the artist, the love that engenders and constitutes a work of art. Significantly, while Terence is talking about art, Rachel is creating it. In 'On Not Knowing Greek' Woolf says Dostoevsky leads us to meaning 'by some astonishing run up the scale of emotions' (*CR* 1, p. 7), and in this scene while Terence proses on about his novel, Rachel runs up the staircase of a sonata:

> While Rachel played the piano, Terence sat near her, engaged, as far as the occasional writing of a word in pencil testified, in shaping the world as it appeared to him now that he and Rachel were going to be married.... There she was, swaying enthusiastically over her music, quite forgetful of him, – but he liked that quality in her. He liked the impersonality which it produced in her.... he observed aloud, 'Women – under the heading Women I've written:
>
> "Not really vainer than men. Lack of self-confidence at the base of most serious faults." ... What do you say, Rachel?'
>
> Rachel said nothing. Up and up the steep spiral of a very late Beethoven sonata she climbed....
>
> 'Again, it's the fashion now to say that woman are more practical and less idealistic than men ... – query, what is meant by masculine term, honour? – what corresponds to it in your sex? Eh?'
>
> Attacking her staircase once more, Rachel again neglected this opportunity of revealing the secrets of her sex. She had, indeed, advanced so far in the pursuit of wisdom that she allowed these secrets to rest undisturbed; it seemed to be reserved for a later generation to discuss them philosophically.
>
> Crashing down a final chord with her left hand, she exclaimed at last, swinging round upon him:
>
> 'No, Terence, it's no good; here am I, the best musician in South America, not to speak of Europe and Asia, and I can't play a note because of you in the room interrupting me every other second.'
>
> 'You don't seem to realise that that's what I've been aiming at for the last half-hour,' he remarked. 'I've no objection to nice simple tunes – indeed, I find them very helpful to my literary composition, but that kind of thing is merely like an unfortunate old dog going round on its hind legs in the rain.' (pp. 298–9)

Terence wants only background music for his attempts to fix the silence with a phrase (and he is not really so different from Rachel's father, who wanted Helen to turn his daughter into a good Tory hostess).[4] Rachel's advance 'in the pursuit of wisdom' is marked by the fact that she doesn't try to 'discuss' her insights. Rachel plays the Silence; Clarissa will arrange it; Lily paint it; Percival be it. Woolf creates no successful *literary* artists, and her works always foreground the gap between what the would-be writers are trying to do and what the text itself is doing; the moments of being are most often granted to the non-verbal characters, and the text itself moves toward realms uncharted by literary art.

In *The Voyage Out* Woolf was already reaching toward the novel of silence; for the author, as for Rachel questioning the meaning of love, 'each word as it came into being seemed to shove itself out into an unknown sea' (p. 176), and in the account of Rachel's death Woolf succeeds in rendering experience beyond the usual reach of language. As Rachel slips out of life Terence hovers in the serene joy of their perfect union:

> she had ceased to breathe. So much the better – this was death. It was nothing; it was to cease to breathe. It was happiness, it was perfect happiness. They had now what they had always wanted to have, the union which had been impossible while they lived. Unconscious whether he thought the words or spoke them aloud, he said, 'No two people have ever been so happy as we have been. No one has ever loved as we have loved.'
>
> (pp. 360–1)

Terence and Rachel's love will suffer no further alteration; it has transcended the 'struggle and desire' she so abhorred, to reach, at last, perfect peace. But one confronts here the ironic conjunction of purity and sterility: this union, now far above all breathing human passion, exists only in the eternal separation of the lovers. Ironically, Terence's decisive 'It was happiness, it was perfect happiness' recalls the 'more happy love! more happy, happy love!' of Keats's cold pastoral on the Grecian Urn. Inevitably, because this moment is not etched in marble, the happiness shatters:

> As he saw the passage outside the room, and the table with the cups and the plates, it suddenly came over him that here was a world in which he would never see Rachel again.
> 'Rachel! Rachel!' he shrieked, trying to rush back to her. But they prevented him and pushed him down the passage and into a

bedroom far from her room. Downstairs they could hear the thud of his feet on the floor, as he struggled to break free; and twice they heard him shout, 'Rachel, Rachel!' (p. 361)

The scene illustrates the distinction between describing and the realising process of naming. After Rachel's death Terence thinks 'No two people have ever been so happy as we have been. No one has ever loved as we have loved' (pp. 360–1). Thus he describes their love, but the effect is slightly bathetic. His claim is that of all lovers, and it merely reminds the reader of how inadequate language is to express a complex of intense emotions, or to capture and convey an individual's character. Only with the anguished 'Rachel! Rachel!', wrung from Terence in the transition to a world devoid of love, does the full meaning of their bond make itself felt. There could hardly be a more worn counter than a person's Christian name, and here distorted into a 'shriek' and a 'shout' one might expect to find it emptied of meaning. Yet most readers will feel on the contrary that Terence's howl is fraught with meaning – and that it transforms the name into much more than a label for the recently deceased individual in the other room. Through the name we feel the pressure of Terence's love for Rachel, and because that love has enabled him to become one with her, what is transmitted is all that Rachel has come to be, fulfilled as she is in their union.

Woolf will more effectively focus later works on a single charged utterance – 'Jacob! Jacob!', 'Mrs Ramsay! Mrs Ramsay!', 'O Death!' – for the cry makes the experience intelligible even though that cry contains almost no logical import. Yet even here, it captures the experience and engages the reader with it in the same instant; the word, previously a sign, has become a channel for feeling. The distinction will make itself felt if one compares the charge here carried by 'Rachel, Rachel!' with the relative flatness of 'No one has ever loved as we have loved': the difference in intensity has little to do with the difference in spoken volume. The scene is the crisis point of the novel, a moment of recognition which brings a flash of meaning that irradiates the whole. The many loose ends in the book (Woolf herself later called it an 'assortment of patches') prevent the scene from being entirely successful in this regard. None the less the reader does grasp, in an instant and more completely, all that has been said so discursively about love and about the elusive nature of reality. And in appreciating this knowledge he or she suddenly sees what Terence and Rachel had so haltingly attempted to describe: how art can communicate the things people don't say, how it can afford one a vision of what is 'behind things', and how it can (as Rachel says of music) 'say all there is to say at once' (p. 212). For this scene, after much preparation, has done all those things.

On a holiday in Italy in September of 1908, a month after writing the letter to Clive Bell quoted above, Woolf encountered a fresco in Perugia that prompted her to distinguish between the art of the painter and her own:

> I look at a fresco by Perugino. I conceive that he saw things grouped, contained in certain and invariable forms . . . all beauty was contained in the momentary appearance of human beings. . . . His fresco seems to me infinitely silent; as though beauty had swum up to the top and stayed there, above every- thing else, speech, paths leading on, relations of brain to brain don't exist.

> As for writing – I want to express beauty too – but beauty (symmetry?) of life and the world, in action. Conflict? – is that it? . . . I attain a different kind of beauty, achieve a symmetry by means of infinite discords, showing all the traces of the mind's passage through the world; achieve in the end, some kind of whole made of shivering fragments; to me this seems the natural process; the flight of the mind. (*OB* i, 138)

As Quentin Bell points out, these notes are rapid and disjointed, yet they embody some of the major concerns of *The Voyage Out* and of Woolf's yet unwritten canon. For Woolf no form was ever 'certain and invariable'; the world always seemed to her, as to Rachel, capable of sudden unpredicated change. More than twenty years later she muses in her diary, 'Now is life very solid or very shifting? I am haunted by the two contradictions' (*D* iii, 218). Until the end of her career she continued to examine the protean nature of reality, exploring it through the delicate and intricate processes of language. The broad concern of 'speech, paths leading on, the relation of brain to brain': whatever is connected with 'the flight of the mind' is probably the least misleading statement of what her works are 'about'.[5] The physical event always remains peripheral: the 'action' and 'conflict' she speaks of is the clash between different

modes of thought, the masculine and the feminine, the logical and
the metaphorical. If after *The Voyage Out* we do not see the tension
quite so patently discussed or meditated upon, it remains a
governing factor in the relations of her characters. And the nature
of words themselves continues to figure prominently as a theme in
her work, culminating in Miss La Trobe's obsessed ruminations on
language. For language bears the imprint of both logical and
metaphorical thought, and it is through language that the flight of
the mind can be made visible, and communication achieved.

'Some kind of whole made of shivering fragments' succinctly
describes *The Waves*, and in a more general way it applies to the
method of all her mature work. However, in *The Voyage Out* she has
not yet fulfilled her boast to 're-form the novel and . . . enclose the
whole'. The reader sympathises with Rachel's contention that,
while 'music goes straight for things . . . saying all there is to say at
once', writing involves too much 'scratching on the match box' (p.
212). One could point to much extraneous scratching in *The Voyage
Out*. But in this first novel Woolf has demonstrated that she can
bring language to the flash point, effecting a swift illumination
which, like music, says many things at once. It is this musical quality
(not the sonic or rhythmic effects that blatantly imitate music) that
she strives for in her later work. In her endeavour to capture the
essence of life, rather than the details of existence, Woolf continues
the struggle begun in *The Voyage Out*: to restore language to its
metaphorical intensity – to transform words from pellets of information into channels for perception – and thereby to net that
elusive reality that lies just on the far side of language.

3

'Kew Gardens' and *Jacob's Room*: Pursuing 'It' and the 'Greek Spirit'

'Lucky it isn't Friday', he observed.
'Why? D'you believe in luck?'
'They make you pay sixpence on Friday'.
'What's sixpence anyway? Isn't it worth sixpence?'
'What's "it" – what do you mean by "it"?'
'O, anything – I mean – you know what I mean.' (pp. 124–5)

The reader knows what the young woman means because the conversation occurs near the close of 'Kew Gardens' and Virginia Woolf has already captured 'it': the essence of the natural and the human world of the garden. From the beginning of her career Woolf had been pursuing the 'uncircumscribed spirit' of life, but she had been frustrated by the methods of conventional fiction. Now, she makes no attempt to deal with 'it' discursively – she does not, as she might have done in *The Voyage Out*, have a pair of sensitive individuals discuss the 'what-ness' of Kew. Neither does she offer straightforward description. The sketch represents the artistic application of Woolf's famous manifesto published only the month before in her essay 'Modern Fiction': 'Life is not a series of gig-lamps symmetrically arranged: life is a luminous halo, a semi-transparent envelope surrounding us from the beginning of consciousness to the end' (*CE* II, 106). In 'Kew Gardens' Woolf does not document the physical scene, she immerses the reader in the atmosphere of the garden.[1]

To glance first at the most obvious strategies of narration, in 'Kew Gardens' Woolf dispenses with the carefully articulated structures of *Night and Day*, the 'scaffolding' as she calls it. There is

32

very little external action here – a series of couples strolls past a flower bed in which a snail is struggling to get past a leaf – and the development seems as 'aimless and irregular' as the movements of the people in the gardens. On closer examination it becomes obvious that the sketch is carefully constructed: there are four couples and among them they constitute a cross-section of social class (middle, upper and lower), age (maturity, old age and youth) and relation (husband and wife, male companions, female friends, lovers); and their appearances are neatly interspersed among four passages which describe the action in the flower bed. Yet this pattern is not insisted upon; the juxtapositions are not abrupt or pointed. As in her later works, the progession of events (the 'series of gig-lamps') has been subordinated to the modulation of emotion, and the ending conveys a sense of resolution more than of narrative conclusion. In the human encounters, too, a similarly understated order obtains. The pleasantly elegiac mood created by the married couple, Eleanor and Simon, gives way to uneasy tension as the old man exhibits a senility that borders on madness. The glimpse of something darker merely hints at the turmoil underlying the tranquil scene (a conjunction of beauty and terror that remains constant in Woolf's writings) before the coarse curiosity of the two women restores the lighter tone. Finally the emotions that the lovers now feel echo those evoked in Eleanor and Simon only by their memories. Thus Woolf quietly comes full circle to end with love, before shifting to a more encompassing vision of unity – the entelechy of all her works – of human beings integrated not just with each other but with the phenomenal world: 'they wavered and sought shade beneath the trees, dissolving like drops of water in the yellow and green atmosphere, staining it faintly with red and blue' (p. 126).

The achieved effect of the sketch, the sense that it is an atmosphere into which one moves, follows in part from the fluid overall structure, but the reader's immersion begins at the outset with the smoothly shifting point of view. Woolf does more than set the scene in the opening paragraph, she smoothly dislocates the reader's accustomed perspective of a landscape. The first sentence, 'From the oval-shaped flower-bed there rose perhaps a hundred stalks' (p. 119), begins with a description from a middle distance; the narrator sees the shape of the bed as a whole, but also sees the flowers as individual entities, not as a solid mass. Yet by the end of the sentence the narrator has moved much closer, to the 'yellow gloom of the throat', from which emerges 'a straight bar, rough with gold dust and slightly clubbed at the end'. And, as the light 'move[s] on and spread[s] its illumination in the *vast* green spaces' (my emphasis) beneath the dome of leaves, the reader has been placed among the flowers and given a correspondingly different sense of scale. As the paragraph closes, the breeze 'over-head' is now above in the petals, not in the trees: 'Then the breeze stirred rather more briskly overhead and the colour was flashed into the air above, into the eyes of the men and women'. We now find ourselves viewing the bed from within – the angle of vision is in fact that of the snail – rather than admiring the floral designs as a more distant observer.

Just as the initial description begins with and then moves beyond a conventional perspective on the scene, so the first exchange between Eleanor and Simon ('"Fifteen years ago I came here with Lily", he thought.... "Tell me, Eleanor. D'you ever think of the past?"') moves out of interior monologue and then, with '"For me, a square silver shoe buckle and a dragon fly –" "For me, a kiss"' (pp. 120–1), into a new mode, one that seems to combine qualities of both thought and speech. Again, Woolf is gently forcing the reader out of his or her established perceptual habits, raising questions about the nature of discourse and the conventions used to render it. And just as she has placed the reader within the garden, so with each successive dialogue she moves deeper, below the flat surface of words, to reveal that, like the apparently flat flower-bed, language too has cliffs and hollows. In doing so she dramatises the way in which one often perceives words less as units of information than as physical sensation.

Indeed, as the two women talk, their words finally cease to have more than vestigial denotative meaning for the 'stout' member of the pair; they become as palpable, and as non-cognitive, as a rain shower: 'The ponderous woman looked through the pattern of falling words at the flowers.... She stood there letting the words fall over her, swaying the top part of her body slowly backwards and forwards, looking at the flowers' (pp. 123–4). The image prepares the reader for the final encounter, that between Trissie and her young man. For after the brief discussion on the cost of admission (quoted at the beginning of this chapter) Woolf moves into their minds, exploring the unvoiced reactions to the colloquy. It is here that the alternation between description and dialogue becomes a fusion, as the words become not merely a 'pattern' but a contoured landscape, and one whose features echo those of the terrain through which the snail has been moving.

In this episode Woolf displays what will become the defining characteristic of her later prose: a flexible narrative style which allows her to move without obvious transition from an external point of view to one within the mind of a character, and back again, thus fusing the physical setting with the perceiving consciousness. Further, it is a mode which invites the reader's participation in the process, so that the reality Woolf conveys is apprehended through the experience of reading. In the passage quoted below, the reader becomes conscious of moving *among* words, just as the characters do.

> Long pauses came between each of these remarks; they were uttered in toneless and monotonous voices. The couple stood still on the edge of the flower bed, and together pressed the end of her parasol deep down into the soft earth. The action and the fact that his hand rested on the top of hers expressed their feelings in a strange way, as these short insignificant words also expressed something, words with short wings for their heavy body of meaning, inadequate to carry *them* far and thus alighting awkwardly upon the very common objects that surrounded *them*, and were to *their* inexperienced touch so massive; but who knows (so they thought as they pressed the parasol into the earth) what precipices aren't concealed in them, or what slopes of ice don't shine in the sun on the other side? Who knows? Who has ever seen this before? Even when she wondered what sort of tea they gave you at Kew, he felt that something loomed up behind her words, and stood vast and solid behind them; and the mist very slowly rose and uncovered – O, Heavens, what were those shapes? – little white tables, and waitresses. (p. 12; emphasis added)

The passage begins straightforwardly enough: the narrator notes the pauses, the tone of the remarks, the posture of the couple. But in the third sentence, as she explores the relation of the words to the feelings they are meant to convey, the narrator draws the reader into the emotions of the couple. The initial image describing the words evolves into an extended metaphor that communicates more exactly the 'something' the young couple feels, and the metaphor works in part through deliberately ambiguous pronouns which both enforce the reader's engagement and unite the disparate elements of the scene.

The words 'with short wings for their heavy body' suggest bees – appropriate both to the garden and to the drone of the 'toneless and monotonous voices' of the speakers. As the passage develops, it sustains this dual reference: 'inadequate to carry them far' seems to refer as easily to the words being inadequate to carry the couple far as it does to the wings being inadequate to carry the words far. The latter proves to be the primary meaning, for the words alight on the 'common objects'. But with 'common objects that surrounded *them*' the pronoun can refer to either the couple or the words. The latter would appear to be the logical choice, yet in the next clause, 'and were to *their* inexperienced touch so massive', the pronoun obviously refers to the couple.

'Massive', however, seems to modify the common objects – in which case 'their' should refer to the words-as-bees – unless the words from the couple's point of view are massive. This seems unlikely (they have been described as 'short, insignificant'), and the following clause, 'but who knows ... what precipices aren't concealed in them', perpetuates the confusion over the pronoun referent, for the reader knows that there are precipices in these common objects; we have already encountered the 'brown cliffs and deep green lakes' (p. 121) that block the snail's path. Nevertheless, the precipices do reside in the words. The image of the bee has somehow fallen by the way, and the young man and woman now look through the words, as the older woman earlier 'looked through the pattern of falling words at the flowers', to the something 'vast and solid' behind the words.

I spoke of confusion, and the passage is confusing if one insists on pinning down all the referents. But through an alert and unprejudiced attention to the syntax, one can more firmly apprehend the action of the figures: what is being fostered is identification, not confusion. The reader does not find the passage muddled; rather he or she experiences the sense of one thing merging with another – the couple with the words, the words with the surrounding objects. And the reader easily makes the transition from bees to precipices, for the one expresses the activity of the conversation, while the other conveys the young man's perception of the meaning behind the words; the massiveness and solidity expressed the intensity of their emotions. Indeed the image of the bee, from 'words with short wings' to 'that surrounded them', can be regarded as a parenthetical aside by the narrator, after which she returns to the consciousness of the young couple. In any case, Woolf's supple prose ensures that while the reader is invited to attend closely he or she is not forced to pause. The impression of a cloudiness or 'mist' that Woolf creates derives from extreme precision, not vagueness, and it conveys exactly that sense lovers have of the world dissolving into soft focus as they become for a moment oblivious of all except each other. Further, the reader experiences the wonder at ordinary objects which follows such intense moments: 'O, Heavens, what were those shapes – little white tables.' Yet by using the most bathetic object available to satisfy that portentous anticipation, Woolf gently puts the event in perspective; the reader feels a sympathetic amusement toward the infatuated couple. He or she continues to identify with them, however, for the shock of wonder is not described, rather it is conveyed through the prose as the reader emerges from the mist of the passage.

In fact, the reader is not yet fully out of the mist, for the tables and waitresses, we gradually discern, have not been observed – they are just now taking shape in the young man's mind:

> O, Heavens, what were those shapes? – little white tables, and waitresses who looked first at her and then at him; and there was a bill that he would pay with a real two shilling piece, and it was real, all real, he assured himself, fingering the coin in his pocket, real to everyone except to him and to her; even to him it began to seem real; and then – but it was too exciting to stand and think any longer, and he pulled the parasol out of the earth with a jerk and was impatient to find the place where one had tea with other people, like other people.   (p. 125)

The touch of the coin brings him back by degrees to the external world – 'even to him it began to seem real' – and the reader too must struggle to regain the conventional sense of the reality of the park. For Woolf has convinced us of what she had so firmly stated in 'Modern Fiction', that life 'is a little other than custom would have us believe it' (CE II, 106). In any case, Woolf does not follow them to tea; the sketch closes with a vision of the human bodies, the flowers, the voices and the traffic noises all dissolving in the heat of the afternoon. The tables, the shilling, the parasol, elements she called 'the alien and external', finally have far less immediacy than what Trissie could only describe as 'it': the 'yellow and green atmosphere' that is both ethos and ambience of the garden.[2]

In her novels Woolf would continue to explore the relation between language and reality – both dramatically, through the experience and conscious probing of her characters, and formally, through the experimental techniques of her works. The quality she called 'life' or the 'essential thing' refused to be fixed by a phrase, but it could be arrested, briefly, by a net of words: words that evoke as well as indicate, that conspire to produce their own luminous halo, rendering (by inducing) a process of consciousness rather than a concrete picture.

In early January of 1920 – the first month of a decade that would come to be identified with literary experiment – Virginia Woolf was excitedly considering 'a new form for a new novel'. She was not yet sure exactly what shape this new work would take, but she knew it would leave behind the traditional form of her two previous novels, *The Voyage Out* and *Night and Day*, and move in the directions suggested by the short sketches she had been writing: 'Suppose one thing should open out of another – as in *An Unwritten Novel*', she wrote in her diary on 26 January, 'only not for 10 pages but 200 or so – doesn't that give the looseness & lightness I want: doesnt that get closer & yet keep form & speed, & enclose everything, everything?' (*D* II, 13). Three months later, on a rainy April morning, she sketched out a plan:

> Reflections upon beginning a work of fiction to be called, perhaps, *Jacob's Room*: Thursday, April 15th 1920
>
> I think the main point is that it should be free.
> Yet what about form?
> Let us suppose that the *Room* will hold it together.
> Intensity of life compared with immobility.
> Experiences.
> To change style at will.[3]

This preliminary note seems to indicate that the focus and the structuring principles were clear in her mind from the outset. But Woolf's intentions were not at all certain: she will 'perhaps' call the book *Jacob's Room*; she says, 'Let us suppose' the room will hold it together. The book was not written simply as an experiment in style, but neither – to take the other extreme – was it conceived as an anti-war polemic. Whether one takes the book to be about a particular young man named Jacob (modelled on Thoby Stephen), or the generation lost in the war (epitomised by a figure who resembles Rupert Brooke), or about the relationship between the narrator and her subject, or about the process of perception and the nature of being, or all of this and more, one finds in the manuscript a gradual, and often very tentative, process of discovery as both the subject matter and the form evolve together. The manuscript reveals that Woolf seemed to be thinking of structuring her novel around the rooms of several characters, not Jacob's alone. However, she came to use 'room' in a less literal, more metaphoric sense: in the published version Jacob's 'room' is his domicile, his psychic space, his society and ultimately the text itself.

The central tension in these various 'rooms' is that between what she calls the 'unseizable force' and 'the Greek spirit', between the violence of institutions and the order produced by art, between a mass impulse and the force of individual inspiration. It is the 'Greek spirit' that governs Jacob's development from his years at university until his moment of ecstasy with Sandra Wentworth Williams on the road to the Acropolis. At Cambridge, Jacob's intimacy with Simeon and, in part, the light of Cambridge are generated by the discussion of Julian the Apostate:

> But intimacy – the room was full of it, still, deep, like a pool. Without need of movement or speech it rose softly and washed over everything, mollifying, kindling, and coating the mind with the lustre of pearl, so that if you talk of a light, of Cambridge burning, it's not languages only. It's Julian the Apostate.
>
> (pp. 43–4)

The reference is pointed. Julian was, like Jacob, a man of ability who died young in war. Further, although trained in Christianity, Julian became so enthralled with Hellenic culture that he attempted to restore the pagan gods. But his was an idealised version, fostered by his teachers, which had never actually existed. Jacob, trained in a similar misconception, is greatly disillusioned with Greece, and the narrator declares,

But it is the governesses who start the Greek myth. . . . First you
read Xenophon; then Euripides. One day – that was an occasion,
by God – what people have said appears to have sense in it; 'the
Greek spirit'; the Greek this, that, and the other. . . . The point is,
however, that we have been brought up in an illusion.   (p. 133)

Jacob is unprepared for modern Greek society, where 'Aristotle' is
a waiter, peripatetic in search of a tip (p. 134), but it is not just that
the Classical age is gone; like Julian he is searching for something
that never really was.

In Jacob's case the illusion is compounded by romantic infatuation. In London he and Timmy Durrant tramp down Haverstock
Hill at dawn after a party, shouting Greek:

it seemed to him that they were making the flagstones ring on the
road to the Acropolis . . . for the whole sentiment of Athens was
entirely after his heart; free, venturesome, high-spirited. . . . She
had called him Jacob without asking his leave. She had sat upon
his knee. Thus did all good women in the days of the
Greeks. (pp. 73–4)

Clearly his exultant cries have more to do with Florinda having sat
on his knee than with an appreciation of Greek culture. (Later, in
an apt deflation, Woolf has Jacob see Florinda turning up 'Greek
Street', a haunt of prostitutes, on another man's arm.) Once in
Greece, although he is disappointed by the temples, Jacob is
enchanted by the pretentious and superficial Sandra, of whom the
narrator says, 'hers was the English type which is so Greek' (p. 138).
But this is a woman who carries Chekhov because it is 'convenient
for travelling', and Balzac because it suits her ensemble, and who
thinks in greeting-card platitudes: '"I am full of love for everyone"
. . . The tragedy of Greece was the tragedy of all high souls. She
seemed to have grasped something. She would write it down'
(p. 137).

However, though the narrator disparages the distortion of the
Greek spirit, she does not deny the spirit itself. The temples on the
Acropolis possess an 'immortal' beauty, a 'spiritual energy' which
endures separate from 'memories, abandonments, regrets, sentimental devotions' (p. 144), and Greek literature is, the narrator
declares, 'a specific; a clean blade; always a miracle' (p. 73). Sandra
is spurious, the *Phaedrus* is not. It is part of the cultural tradition, of

the 'vast mind' enshrined in the British Museum (p. 105). Jacob, in solitary study, achieves a genuine communion with the work:

> The *Phaedrus* is very difficult. And so, when at length one reads straight ahead, falling into step, marching on, becoming (so it seems) momentarily part of this rolling, imperturbable energy, which has driven darkness before it since Plato walked the Acropolis, it is impossible to see to the fire. . . . Plato's argument is stowed away in Jacob's mind, and for five minutes Jacob's mind continues alone, onwards, into the darkness.   (p. 106)

There is still a gentle irony here, for the dialogue deals with problems of rhetoric and love, and the relations between the spiritual and the sensual, issues that Jacob will face not in the abstract but in the flesh when he encounters Sandra in Greece, and walks with her to the Acropolis (pp. 156–7). Nevertheless, this approach to the Acropolis is different from the enthusiasm on Haverstock Hill, and it is clear the narrator believes there is a cultural spirit that can be transmitted through the ages.[4] Jacob may be wrong-headed, but (as with Paul and Minta, the lovers in *To the Lighthouse*), his idealism is both foolish and glorious; his sense that there is something better than a world governed by commerce is to be admired. However, there is another force operating upon Jacob, that which ultimately destroys him.

For the politicians and businessmen it is not the Greek spirit but a certain 'unseizable force' (which novelists never manage to capture) that is the vital spirit of civilisation: it is the 'incessant commerce' of banks and other institutions that 'oars the world forward'. The narrator introduces the force in a digression on gossip, presenting the 'highly respectable opinion that character-mongering is much overdone these days':

> So we are driven back to see what the other side means – the men in clubs and Cabinets – when they say that character drawing is a frivolous fireside art, a matter of pins and needles, exquisite outlines enclosing vacancy, flourishes, and mere scrawls.
>
> (pp.150–1)

At first the narrator seems to be scorning these 'gossips' who 'stuff out their victims' characters till they are swollen and tender' (pp. 150–1). But after giving the board-room opinion, she shifts without comment to a vignette of technological warfare:

> The battleships ray out over the North Sea ... a dozen young
> men in the prime of life descend with composed faces into the
> depths of the sea; and there impassively (though with perfect
> mastery of machinery) suffocate uncomplainingly together.
>
> (p. 151)

When she comes back to the question of character, after the
nonchalant deaths of young men, it is to say that 'the novelists' (not
'character-mongers' now) never catch the 'unseizable force'. Further, it is not the narrator who expresses these opinions. As we are
told, with a phrase at first innocuous but finally bitterly ironic, it is
'they' – the men in the clubs and Cabinets – who 'say' these things:

> *they say* that character-drawing is a frivolous fireside art....
> These actions [the engagements of war], together with the
> incessant commerce of banks, laboratories, chancellories, and
> houses of business, are the strokes which oar the world forward,
> *they say*. ...
>   It is thus that we live, *they say*, driven by an unseizable force.
> *They say* that the novelists never catch it, that it goes hurtling
> through their nets and leaves them torn to ribbons. This, *they say*
> is what we live by – this unseizable force. (pp. 151–2; emphasis
> added)

Those who would draw character now appear superior to those
who would so efficiently obliterate it. Woolf is deepening the
political satire, suggesting that the impulse to create character is
not as frivolous as it seems, that in fact the 'fireside art', be it gossip
or scrawls, is an ordering force (and a force of love, we know from
the activity of the narrator herself), which runs counter to the
'unseizable' will to power, and which belies what 'they say', that this
is all we live by. Indeed, the force is counter to life: when the
policeman at Ludgate Circus raises his arm,

> all the force in his veins flows straight from shoulder to finger-
> tips; not an ounce is diverted into sudden impulses, sentimental
> regrets, wire-drawn distinctions. (p. 152)

'Sudden impulses, sentimental regrets' recalls the passage a few pages earlier on the beauty of the Pathenon, which endures apart from 'abandonments, regrets, sentimental devotions', and the echo brings the two forces into sharp juxtaposition: the 'Greek spirit' transcends humanity; the 'unseizable force' debases humanity.

Yet this force, too, seems to be somehow connected with the developing friendship between Jacob and Sandra: at the same time as the guests at Mrs Durrant's are talking about guns and Germany, 'Jacob (driven by this unseizable force) walked rapidly down Hermes Street and ran straight into the Williamses' (p. 152). That this unseizable force which raises the pillars of the establishment and leads to war should be the same impulse that drives Jacob to Sandra might seem curious at first. But it is not the force of the institutions themselves, but desire channelled through the institutions. It is the creative force in its dark aspect, the will to mate and dominate that appears again in the mad fecundity of the 'Time Passes' section of *To the Lighthouse*, or in the mingled lust and aggression that underlies the sexual and military politics of *Between the Acts*.

The counter agent to the 'unseizable force' – or more properly the other side of it, for the two are not ultimately separable – is the 'Greek spirit'. It is a spirit which links, like the letters without which our lives would 'split asunder' (p. 89), like the conversations which create a 'spiritual shape' (p. 43), and like the art of character-drawing, forging something absolute though intangible. In short, it is this force, illusive and elusive as it is, which creates civilisation, and it is the 'unseizable force' that rips like bullets through the nets of the novelists, which threatens to destroy society. The narrator sees what Jacob does not, that inspired idealism and crude acquisitiveness are both present in the raw energy of society. Civilisation is neither the pure design created by Jacob's Cambridge tutors, nor the embodiment of Commerce envisioned by the men in clubs and Cabinets. Jacob, like Julian before him, would like to preserve the Greek ethos unsullied by its base elements. His mistake is in thinking he can keep them separate. He equates Sandra with one of the caryatids on the Erechtheum (p. 147) – but he is probably looking at the terracotta replacement of the one taken by Lord Elgin and placed in the British Museum. Aesthetics and imperialism, the Greek spirit and the unseizable force, are all intertwined.

The image which unites them both, and joins them with Jacob's character, is the wind. The breeze (traditionally associated with inspiration) appears after the conversation at Cambridge about Julian the Apostate:

> 'Julian the Apostate . . .' Which of them said that and the other words murmured round it? But about midnight there sometimes rises, like a veiled figure suddenly woken, a heavy wind; and this now flapping through Trinity lifted unseen leaves and blurred everything.   (p. 43)

The wind rises again as Sandra and Jacob approach the Acropolis:

> Violent was the wind now rushing down the Sea of Marmara between Greece and the plains of Troy. . . . Sandra's veils were swirled about her.   (p. 156)

The wind swirling Sandra's veils associates her with the veiled figure at Cambridge, and that ambiguous light of civilisation. But now the wind links the lights of modern European civilisation, lights, in an action symbolic of the preparation for war, that are going out:

> Now the agitation of the air uncovered a racing star. Now it was dark. Now one after another lights were extinguished. Now the great towns – Paris – Constantinople – London – were black as strewn rocks.   (p. 156)

Finally, the breeze is linked to the snuffing out of Jacob's light. A gust stirs the leaves (as it had at Trinity) as Bonamy looks out Jacob's window:

> And then suddenly all the leaves seemed to raise themselves.
>   'Jacob! Jacob!' cried Bonamy, standing by the window. The leaves sank down again.   (pp. 172–3)

The wind blows teasingly all through this book, at once an emblem of the creative spirit, of the destructive force of aggression and of the unknowable quality the narrator is trying to catch in Jacob's character.

Unlike the leisurely *Voyage Out* or the voluminous *Night and Day*, *Jacob's Room* is pared close to the bone. Much of the compression comes from the fact that where she described in her earlier novels, she now dramatises. She reduces authorial comment and exposition, letting her scenes suggest and forcing her reader to make the connections. In the changes between the manuscript and the published text, one can see Woolf working toward a more elliptical style. For instance, when the Reverend Floyd proposes to Jacob's mother she is annoyed, and the manuscript is very explicit about the cause of her distress:

> 'How could I think of marriage!' she thought to herself almost bitterly as the fastened the latch with a piece of wire. It was, probably, that the idea of copulation had now become infinitely remote from her. She did not use the word; & yet as she sat darning the boys clothes that night it annoyed her to find that it was so 'And I dislike red headed men' she said; pushing away her work basket. (MS 1, 23)

In the final version the reader is given only the patently irrelevant detail of red hair and left to infer the real cause of her reluctance:

> 'How could I think of marriage!' she said to herself bitterly, as she fastened the gate with a piece of wire. She had always disliked red hair in men, she thought, thinking of Mr Floyd's appearance, that night when the boys had gone to bed.   (p. 18)

Looking back on the incident as she strokes the cat, she thinks,

> how she had had him gelded & how she did not like red headed men – both thoughts coming on top of each other & making her smile, though she had not used the word gelded or – indeed she never used words when she thought indecent thoughts. Smiling she went into the kitchen . . . . (MS 1, 27)

In the published text the commentary is omitted; she thinks,

> how she had had him gelded, and how she did not like red hair in men. Smiling she went into the kitchen. (p. 20)

In the novel Woolf lets the co-ordinate structure make the connection for us; instead of telling us Betty doesn't put thoughts into words, she dramatises the mental evasion. Further, in the scenes dealing with Jacob's infatuation with Clara, and later with Sandra, Woolf again revises so that the cross-currents of emotion are only hinted at. The manuscript takes us into Jacob, stating his emotions, where the published text regards him exclusively from the outside, engaging us in the narrator's quest to know Jacob.

However, it is the space breaks on the page which constitute the most obvious departure from Woolf's earlier books. These gaps invite the participation of the reader at the same time as they frustrate it, for they make problematic the traditional assumptions about causality. The breaks unite the formal and the thematic aspects of the novel, emphasising that life's connectedness is perhaps only apparent and accidental, that the most ordinary moment is fraught with myriad possibilities. The effect is to challenge the fundamental principles that shape the text itself. In terms of plot the novel is a *bildungsroman*, presenting the growth and development of Jacob, but structurally it denies the implications of that form.[5]

The map of our existence is full of gaps. As the narrator says, 'The streets of London have their map; but our passions are uncharted', and she goes on to suggest the possibilities of, for instance, stopping to listen to the old man on a Holborn street corner instead of brushing by. One could wind up, the narrator says, sketching a chain of events, an

> outcast from civilization, for you have committed a crime, are infected with yellow fever as likely as not, and – fill in the sketch as you like.
>
> As frequent as street corners in Holborn are these chasms in the continuity of our ways. Yet we keep straight on.   (p. 93)

'Life', Woolf said in her diary as she was working on *Jacob's Room*, 'is so like a little strip of pavement over an abyss' (*D* ii, 72), and that sensation is rendered by the space breaks in the text, as well as by the events of Jacob's life.

The events, too, are often deliberately shaped to reinforce this sense of the 'chasms in our ways'. At the finish of the episode in which Jacob and Jinny and the sculptor Cruttendon walk in the gardens at Versailles, Woolf takes them back to the railway station for a sentimental parting:

> They had to separate. . . . the other two were turning away,

though Jinny looked over her shoulder, and Cruttendon, waving his hand, disappeared like the very great genius that he was.   (p. 126)

In the manuscript, the narrator sums up, 'And they never met again' (MS II, 157); for the published version, Woolf ended with action (Cruttendon disappearing) rather than comment, leaving the moment frozen in process. The technique is similar to the cinematic device of the 'freeze-frame': the action stops and after a pause a new action begins. In the novel the blank space on the page provides the moment of suspension.

Again, when Sandra and Jacob take their evening walk to the Acropolis, in the manuscript Woolf has them reaching the Parthenon and agonising over whether or not to kiss (MS II, 267). In the published version the narrator leaves them en route and observes, almost offhandedly, 'As for reaching the Acropolis who shall say that we ever do it, or that when Jacob woke next morning he found anything hard and durable to keep for ever?' (p. 160). Further, in working over the conclusion Woolf once more altered to achieve the effect of action suspended, broken off. She first wrote,

'What is one to do with these, Mr Bonamy?'
She held out a pair of Jacob's old shoes.
[They both laughed]
[The room waved behind her tears.]   (MS III, 63)

Left at the end the tears would have provided a resolution of the action, shifting the focus to the mother's grief. By breaking in mid-action Woolf emphasises the impossibility of making sense of such a death; the closing leaves the reader with the absence which swallows Bonamy's cry, 'Jacob! Jacob!' The waving of the external world behind Betty's tears was shifted to the beginning of the novel where it introduces the united themes of perception and mortality.

Finally, the gaps are part of the text's own questioning of itself. The narrator laments the fact that language has a tendency to slide away from one's grasp: 'Even the exact words get the wrong accent on them' (p. 70). And she does not want to transmit facts: 'of all futile occupations this of cataloguing features is the worst' (p. 68). The problem is that

words have been used too often; touched and turned, and left

exposed to the dust of the street. The words we seek hang close
to the tree. We come at dawn and find them sweet beneath the
leaf.   (p. 90)

The narrator is conscious of how often both written and spoken
communication go awry: Florinda's guileless hand disguises an
unfaithful nature (p. 91); Mrs Flanders cannot say the things she
really wants to (p. 87); Jacob's letters to her from Europe are
misleading (pp. 123, 127, 135), while those to Bonamy simply do
not get written (p. 143). Yet with letters 'at last the power of the
mind to quit the body is manifest', and, the narrator insists,

> Life would split asunder without them. 'Come to tea, come to
> dinner, what's the truth of the story? have you heard the news?
> . . . These are our stays and props. These lace our days together
> and make of life a perfect globe.   (p. 89)

Indeed, words occasionally do create a 'perfect globe'. When Jacob
and Simeon talk, they achieve 'the intimacy, a sort of spiritual
suppleness, when mind prints upon mind indelibly' (p. 43). It is this
same phenomenon of 'mind printing upon mind' that Jacob
experiences when he reads the *Phaedrus*. And it is this that the
narrator is trying to achieve in her account of Jacob, to engage the
audience, to make us fill in the gaps and at the same time recognise
that they can never conclusively be bridged.

Nevertheless most readers feel that Woolf does not really suc-
ceed in bringing us to an intimate knowledge of Jacob, however
much she succeeds in dramatising the narrator and her quest, or
examining the cultural forces that shape Jacob (indeed, in many
ways *Jacob's Room* anticipates the postmodernist practices of *Between
the Acts*). She has not yet fulfilled her prophecy in 'The Mark on the
Wall' (1917) that the novelist of the future will turn from 'that shell
of a person which is seen by other people' to explore the 'depths'
beneath (pp. 112–13). In *Mrs Dalloway* Woolf probes beneath the
surface, 'digging out beautiful caves behind my characters', as she
puts it (*D*, ɪɪ, 263), and she develops a style closer to that of the
sketches, moving from her choppiest book to what would be her
most fluid. In *Jacob's Room* the narrator speaks of how letters can
make a 'perfect globe'; in *Mrs Dalloway* Woolf fashions such a globe.

4
Mrs Dalloway: Writing, Speech and Silence

In *Mrs Dalloway* Virginia Woolf found her voice, a voice that moves effortlessly in and out of the minds of the characters, absorbing the myriad individual voices, a voice that lies like a film over the whole novel, not only uniting it but *becoming* it so that, unlike in *Jacob's Room*, the action of the narrative is inseparable from the action of the voice. The narrator performs a function analogous to that of Clarissa as hostess, and Clarissa's theory of connection, that 'she survived . . . being laid out like a mist between the people she knew best, who lifted her on their branches as she had seen the trees lift the mist, but it spread ever so far, her life, herself' (p. 10), is a theory that governs not only events of the narrative but the functions of the prose. The intricacies of free indirect discourse have been amply documented,[1] but it is the way in which the voice engages the reader, implicating him or her in the rhythms of the novel, that concerns me here, that and the related consideration of how the functions of language constitute a major theme of the novel, and, more generally and more speculatively, how questions about the priority of writing and speech help define the particular quality of the discourse in *Mrs Dalloway*. For it seems to me that the novel hovers – or more accurately, oscillates – between the two, even as it ultimately locates meaning and presence in silence.

Critics have noted how the characters are linked by 'collective images', and further how these characters seem to be not so much connected with each other as absorbed by the narrating consciousness, which distills and renders their experience. Yet there are connections more subtle still. James Naremore points out that when Peter is in Regent's Park the 'rhythmic pulse we feel in Peter's thought . . . is emphasized by the repetitions in the paragraph describing Rezia's thought; so that the inner lives of these two

49

characters, who are very different (she is a foreigner) and who do not know one another, seem attuned to the same elemental beat'.[2] Naremore cites but does not analyse the passage, yet his assertion that rhythms as well as images link the characters is worth exploring. The rhythm that pervades the novel has been described by Hillis Miller, who observes that the two contrary movements of the novel, the rising, constructive action that culminates in the party, and the falling movement, the disintegration and final plunge into death of Septimus, are embodied in the opening of the third paragraph of the novel: 'What a lark! What a plunge!' Further, he points out that the characters live according to an abrupt nervous rhythm, 'rising one moment to heights of ecstasy only to be dropped again in sudden terror or despondency'.[3] Thus not only the overriding movement of the novel but the psychic rhythms of the characters which together constitute that movement are organised around rising and falling.

In the following passage, an early scene between Rezia and Septimus in Regent's Park, one can see how Woolf incorporates these rhythms and how they engage the reader. The passage also reveals how the author interweaves the two related but distinct narrative lines of Septimus and Clarissa, making the moment when the paths of the two characters intersect seem, if not inevitable, at least not arbitrary. Because the passage is quite long I have inserted virgules to assist the reader in following the subsequent discussion:

'For you should see the Milan gardens,' she said aloud. But to whom?

There was nobody. Her words faded. So a rocket fades. Its sparks, having grazed their way into the night, surrender to it, dark descends, pours over the outlines of houses and towers; bleak hill-sides soften and fall in. But though they are gone, the night is full of them; robbed of colour, blank of windows, they exist more ponderously, give out what the frank daylight fails to transmit – the trouble and suspense of things conglomerated there in the darkness; huddled together in the darkness; / reft of the relief which dawn brings when, washing the walls white and grey, spotting each window-pane, lifting the mist from the fields, showing the red-brown cows peacefully grazing, all is once more decked out to the eye; exists again. / I am alone; I am alone! she cried, by the fountain in Regent' Park (staring at the Indian and his cross), as perhaps at midnight, when all boundaries are lost,

the country reverts to its ancient shape, as the Romans saw it,
lying cloudy, when they landed, and the hills had no names and
rivers wound they knew not where – such was her darkness; /
when suddenly, as if a shelf were shot forth and she stood on it,
she said how she was his wife, married years ago in Milan, his
wife, and would never, never tell that he was mad! Turning, the
shelf fell; down, down she dropped. For he was gone, she
thought – gone, as he threatened, to kill himself – to throw
himself under a cart! But no; there he was; still sitting alone on
the seat, in his shabby overcoat, his legs crossed, staring, talking
aloud.   (p. 23)

Woolf first draws the reader into the passage through deliberately
equivocal pronouns. Rezia's words fade like sparks in the night, a
night which falls over the hillsides and the outlines of houses and
towers. Woolf then begins to extend her image: 'But though they
are gone, the night is full of them'. Although the proper antecedent of 'they' is 'hillsides', the statement applies equally to the hills,
the outlines of the houses, or the sparks. 'Sparks' is at this point still
uppermost in our minds, but in fact Woolf is moving beyond the
original figure and into the scene created to amplify it. The next
phrase, 'robbed of colour', sustains the identification of hills and
sparks (and houses, although we would be less likely to associate
colour with 'outlines of houses'); but the rest of the clause, 'blank of
windows, they exist more ponderously', shifts the focus specifically
to the houses and towers. The sparks, and with them the last link
with Rezia's words, have been forgotten. Yet Rezia's emotion is
being ever more precisely conveyed, for the ominousness of the
houses and towers, which imparts the 'trouble and suspense' of
things that the 'frank daylight' disguises, corresponds to Septimus's
outwardly calm silence.

The sentence itself seems to have led us into 'suspense' and
'trouble'; the direction is obscure and progress slows as the prose
coagulates around the heavy vowels and obstructive consonants of
'things conglomerated there in the darkness; huddled together in
the darkness'. With the repetition of 'in the darkness' we come
almost to a standstill. This marks the nadir, for immediately the
semantic gloom begins to lift. With 'walls' and 'window panes' we
can be certain of what we are dealing with, and the relief that dawn
brings is further transmitted through a quickening in the prose. It
moves swiftly on the easy flow of present participles.

washing the walls ... spotting each window-pane ... lifting the
mist ... showing the red-brown cows grazing

a flow augmented by alliteration,

reft of relief ... washing walls white ... from fields

and then also by internal rhymes,

lifting the mist ... red-brown cows.

Also, in descending into the darkness we did so step by step, on
sentence members predominantly discrete, with each detail developing but not implied by the one before. The description of the
dawn comes as a dramatic contrast: the periodic clause holds our
attention (an anticipation unlike our previous 'suspense') as it swells
to an almost festive conclusion – 'all is once more decked out'. The
source of this glad relief is then given a sharp focus in the final
apposition: 'all is once more decked out to the eye; exists again'.
Not the colours, nor the peacefulness of the scene, but 'existence' is
cause for celebration. The importance of the distinction declares
itself later when it is revealed that Clarissa's 'gift' is the ability
simply 'to be, to exist' (p. 154). The complicated image has led away
from the particulars of the scene in the park for a purpose: in
order that the pure quality of existence may be isolated and
emphasised. And in fact, a direct connection is only deferred. The
windows, the sun and the beauty of existence itself later come
together when the present situation reaches its crisis, and Septimus, perched on the window-ledge with his last thoughts, waits 'to
the very last moment. He did not want to die. Life was good. The
sun hot' (p. 132).

The narrator returns to Rezia with 'I am alone; I am alone! she
cried', bringing the reader down with a sudden jolt, to realise that
he or she had not left the darkness at all. (Thus we participate in
the abrupt nervous rhythms Miller discovers in the characters.)
The description of the dawn has only made vivid what this scene so
utterly lacks. The darkened land is now empty, and the sense of
vague menace is replaced by disorientation:

all boundaries are lost, the country reverts to its ancient shape, as
the Romans saw it, lying cloudy, when they landed, and the hills
had no names and rivers wound they knew not where – such was
her darkness.

The figure aptly expresses Rezia's bewilderment in her new country, and, more particularly, the passage emphasises how little she resembles her adventurous ancestors, how much she depends upon her husband. Her marriage is the precarious 'shelf' on which she stands, and which drops when she thinks of Septimus's death (participating vicariously beforehand, as Clarissa will after the fact, in his plunge):

> suddenly, as if a shelf were shot forth and she stood on it, she said how she was his wife.... Turning, the shelf fell; down, down, she dropped. For he was gone, she thought – gone, as he threatened, to kill himself.

The image gains in impact because we ourselves have already experienced an abrupt drop from the plenitude of life to barren isolation in crossing the sentence break: 'all is once more decked out to the eye; exists again. I am alone; I am alone! she cried'.

This section again demonstrates the close interweaving of the strands of the novel. The drop foreshadows Septimus's drop out of existence from the window-ledge of the boarding house. And, when Rezia's rising hysteria is checked by the sight of Septimus, the words, 'But no; there he was; still sitting', anticipate the novel's final line, which marks the moment when Peter looks up to see Clarissa: 'For there she was;'. (The semicolon after 'was' emphasises the integrity of the clause and thus enhances the echo between the passages. The connection is lost if one substitutes a comma: 'But no; there he was, still sitting alone on the seat, in his shabby overcoat'.) The correspondence increases, in retrospect or on a second reading, the pathos of this scene in the park, for Peter's is a moment of joy and completion where Rezia's is but a temporary reprieve. Even the feelings of 'terror' and 'ecstasy' which Peter feels as Clarissa approaches seem to mock Rezia's predicament: she is overcome with terror, and the only hint of ecstasy is her intense relief that Septimus has not yet killed himself. Further, the fulness of Clarissa's presence highlights the bitter irony of the qualifications that follow 'there he was': 'But not; there he was; still sitting alone on the seat, in his shabby overcoat, his legs crossed, staring, talking aloud'. He exists only as a shell. The vignette of Septimus in his vacant isolation, talking aloud but to no one, defines by antithesis the wordless communion between Peter and Clarissa at the close of the book.

Thus this one fragment embodies the two intersecting movements of the novel. The first long passage ('So a rocket fades ... exists again') traces a course down into a troubled darkness and then up into the light, to an affirmation of life. This section is not linked explicitly, as is the subsequent one, to Rezia's mood; indeed one could move directly from 'Her words faded' to 'I am alone' without a sense of omission. But while the first passage does bear upon Rezia's situation, it also broadly outlines the course Clarissa follows, from disillusionment through a vicarious death to renewal or rebirth. The second passage ('I am alone ... staring, talking aloud') moves into a darkness which this time is only fitfully relieved. It more deliberately expresses Rezia's emotions ('such was her darkness'), and it specifically indicates the path of Septimus's inexorable decline to the point where he goes, 'as he threatened, to kill himself'. This, of course, is the death in which Clarissa participates.

I have had to be overly explicit in order to make the patterns and cross-references clear, but I do not suggest that Woolf carefully diagrammed this passage before writing, nor that one would consciously make all these connections on a first reading. Nevertheless, the echo of 'there she was' is clearly deliberate, for the manuscript reveals that the scene was written *after* the conclusion had been drafted.[4] And the section does display specific links which serve to unite one scene with another and to blend the two narrative lines; it also embodies the rise and fall which constitutes the fundamental rhythm of the novel. Although the cross-referencing may not be quite as dense in all passages, this scene is not unique; the web of relation is sustained throughout.

The novel engages the reader in the rhythms of the prose but it invites an intellectual engagement with words as well, for even characterisation and plot turn on questions of language. What is surprising, if one drops back and begins to accumulate evidence out of context, is the degree to which the characters are defined by their attitudes toward literature and language. Bradshaw actively resents those who read: 'There was in Sir William, who had never had time for reading, a grudge, deeply buried, against cultivated people who came into his room and intimated that doctors, whose profession is a constant strain upon all the highest faculties, are not educated men' (p. 87). And Holmes, as he advises Septimus to take up some hobby, 'opened Shakespeare – *Antony and Cleopatra*; pushed Shakespeare aside' (p. 82). At the luncheon party are those who are indifferent to literature. Lady Bruton has this 'isle of men' in her blood 'without reading Shakespeare' (p. 160); indeed she remains resolutely unliterary: 'There was a vine, still bearing, which either Lovelace or Herrick – she never read a word of poetry herself, but so the story ran – had sat under' (p. 94). The brisk Hugh Whitebread, whose pompous phrasings for *The Times* are as hollow as his profession, is dismissed by Sally Seton as one who has 'read nothing, thought nothing, felt nothing' (p. 66). The triplet implies a reciprocal relation.

Reading instructs one in how to think and feel, but it is also those who feel intensely who are interested in literature. Richard Dalloway, although superior to Hugh and Lady Bruton in intellect and sensibility, is none the less judged by his own judgement on Shakespeare's sonnets: 'Seriously and solemnly Richard Dalloway got on his hind legs and said that no decent man ought to read Shakespeare's sonnets because it was like listening at keyholes (besides the relationship was not one that he approved). No decent man ought to let his wife visit a deceased wife's sister' (p. 68). His position marks him less as a Philistine than a prude, and it is this that makes him less threatening and more attractive to Clarissa than the literate and passionate Peter Walsh (in any case, Clarissa's most cherished sexual experience is Sally's kiss). Significantly, Richard's only literary ambition is to write a history of Lady Bruton's family (p. 99).

Peter and Sally, who were destined to write have not done so, but their lives are conditioned by books, and Peter's pipedream is still to 'poke about in the Bodleian, and get at the truth about one or two little matters that interested him' (p. 140). Peter knows more than anyone else in their circle about Pope and Addison, for instance, and his passion for books is inseparable from his passion for life. Though Clarissa acknowledges that Peter shaped her – 'She owed him words: "sentimental", "civilized"; they started up every day of her life, as if he guarded her' (p. 34) – she shrinks from him, and the measure of her revulsion is that she can associate him with Kilman:

> Love destroyed too. Everything that was fine, everything that was true went. ... Think of Peter in love – he came to see her after all these years, and what did he talk about? Himself. Horrible passion! she thought. Degrading passion! she thought, thinking of Kilman and her Elizabeth walking to the Army and Navy Stores. (p. 113)

Peter's vital curiosity and Kilman's desiccated intellectualism are poles apart, but they are equally threatening to Clarissa; both seem to violate the 'privacy of the soul' (p. 113). Although she quotes from *Cymbeline*, it is Baron Marbot's memoirs that are her bedside reading – a volume that seems more appropriate to Kilman's reading list than Peter's. As Beverley Schlack has pointed out, the retreat from Moscow that Marbot describes is an apt metaphor for Clarissa's retreat from sexuality.[5]

Septimus enacts in a more extreme way the progress of Clarissa. He has been formed by literature, and he goes to France to save an England that consists 'almost entirely of Shakespeare's plays and Miss Isabel Pole in a green dress walking in a square' (p. 77). In his madness (a reaction not only to the war but to his homosexuality) he repudiates Shakespeare: 'That boy's business of the intoxication of language – *Antony and Cleopatra* – had shrivelled utterly' (p. 79). And with the shrivelling of the delight in language comes a revulsion from the body: 'How Shakespeare loathed humanity – the putting on of clothes, the getting of children, the sordidity of the mouth and the belly!' (p. 79). Rezia, on the other hand, expresses a desire to have a son and to learn to read Shakespeare (p. 80). It becomes clear that a character's reading is not merely an indicator of his or her intellectual status. Indeed, that is probably its least prominent function. Rather, Woolf makes a character's attitude toward literature a measure of the extent to which he or she shrinks from or embraces life in all its varied aspects – physical, emotional and sensual, as well as intellectual.

It is logical that this should be so, for throughout the novel (and her entire canon) Woolf explores the non-intellectual capabilities of language. The voice, for Septimus, has creative power. As he watches the aeroplane, the nursemaid's voice rasps his spine and sends waves of sound running up into his brain, sparking an illumination: 'A marvellous discovery indeed – that the human voice in certain atmospheric conditions (for one must be scientific, above all scientific) can quicken trees into life!' The trees beckon to him, the leaves seem to be 'connected by millions of fibres with his own body ... when the branch stretched he, too, made that statement' (pp. 21–2). What for Clarissa remains an abstract theory of connection ('she survived ... laid out like a mist between the people she knew best, who lifted her on their branches as she had seen the trees lift the mist') becomes for Septimus an experiential truth. As always, Clarissa and Septimus are not far apart; her metaphor and his metamorphosis are not transformations of a different order. At her parties she is trying to create the 'atmospheric conditions' that will effect unity. The ideal is the kind of pre-literate communications/communion represented by the street singer who sings of love that has lasted 'through all ages – when the pavement was grass, when it was swamp, through the age of tusk and mammoth, through the age of silent sunrise' (p. 73). In all of Woolf's novels, from *The Voyage Out* in which Rachel discovers the ability of words to 'drive roads back to the very beginning of the world', uniting people of 'all times and countries' (*VO*, 175) to *Between the Acts* where the words of Miss La Trobe's yet-to-be-written play rise from the primaeval mud, there is always an instance of language's ability to achieve its original fusion with experience. This originary presence is what Woolf leads toward in her novels, and what Clarissa in her desire to 'go much deeper' is striving for through her parties.

Social language and the incantatory moans of the street singer would seem to be at opposite ends of the linguistic spectrum, but they create the conditions for communication in a similar way. Whereas language for Bradshaw is nothing but a data link, in these other forms language becomes a means to orient the flow of unspoken understanding. It is the very triviality of parlour language that constitutes its virtue, for it remains clear to both parties that the denotative meaning is irrelevant, and that speech is being used as gesture. Peter feels Clarissa gives parties merely to impose herself, Richard that she does it to indulge in the excitement, but, she insists, 'both were quite wrong. What she liked was simply life':

> But to go deeper . . . what did it mean to her, this thing she called life? Oh, it was very queer. Here was So-and-so in South Kensington; some one up in Bayswater; and somebody else, say, in Mayfair. And she felt quite continuously a sense of their existence; and she felt what a waste; and she felt what a pity; and she felt if only they could be brought together; so she did it. And it was an offering; to combine, to create; but to whom?
>
> An offering for the sake of offering, perhaps. Anyhow, it was her gift. Nothing else had she of the slightest importance; could not think, write, even play the piano.   (pp. 108–9)

The litany of 'And she felt . . . and she felt . . . and she felt . . . and she felt . . . so she did it' insists upon the instinctiveness of Clarissa's impulse, and further, it directs us to the way in which the process works, through words functioning as rhythm and sound rather than as pellets of information. In *The Voyage Out*, Terence, after an unsatisfactory discussion with a lady, wonders savagely, 'Why was it that relations between different people were so unsatisfactory, so fragmentary, so hazardous, and words so dangerous that the instinct to sympathise with another human being was an instinct to be examined carefully and probably crushed?' (*VO*, 194). Clarissa is less impatient than Terence and more confident of the power of words to make some whole of the fragments that constitute human relations. She is no writer, but language is finally the medium of her creation.

Initially she and Peter feel separate from the gathering and estranged from each other. Gradually, however, the stiffness begins to melt, and Clarissa, like a 'mermaid' in her element reflects the transformation: 'Lolloping on the waves and braiding her tresses she seemed, having that gift still; to be; to exist; to sum it all up in the moment as she passed ... all with the most perfect ease and air of a creature floating in its element' (p. 154). The 'element' is language. As I said earlier, Clarissa is creating the atmosphere that quickens human beings (rather than trees) into life. She creates an atmosphere in the figurative sense of 'mood', but the parties also generate a literal atmosphere – that of sound. The sense of bonding comes about in the communal hum. The signal that the party is becoming a whole is Ralph Lyon's action of beating back the curtain to go on talking, immersed in conversation (p. 151). The exchange between Clarissa and the professor ('"But the noise!" she said. "The noise!" "The sign of a successful party". Nodding urbanely, the Professor stepped delicately off') along with her reflection on the charming but mute young couple ('Not that *they* added perceptibly to the noise of the party' (p. 157) emphasise the importance of sound.[6] Clarissa's apology '"I had meant to have dancing"' (p. 157), underlines the point. The dance, traditionally a symbol of harmony and unity, is here regarded as a lesser alternative, for those incapable of conversation.

The rhythm we have spoken of, in and out, up and down, a restless movement between contraries, exists in the language, which constantly directs us by some sharp observation to the world beyond words and yet just as constantly recalls us to the surface of the prose, to the play of language itself. Woolf held no formal theory of language, but would have found congenial Wittgenstein's contention that there are a variety of fits between language, thought and reality. Indeed, in the manuscripts and in her reported conversation language often seems to have had for her a tangential relation to reality. From a point at which word and object seem to be linked in the traditional form of signification, she departs, moving in a line that, with its own internal logic, diverges further and further from the object, governed less by things than by language's own laws.[7] This is free play that could become terrifying. It does for Septimus, and Woolf herself speaks of metaphors that 'rise up and stalk eyeless and majestic', recognising that language contains a power to transport in ways that we would not wish or choose (*CE* i, 7). It is as if in the act of playing with words one may fiddle with the delicate connection that ties them to things, and once that is loosed be borne away by language.

Watching the skywriting, Septimus sees the letters as signals and then, in a smooth unconscious shift, as themselves the signallers:

> So, thought Septimus, looking up, they are signalling to me. Not indeed in actual words; that is, he could not read the language yet; but it was plain enough, this beauty, this exquisite beauty, and tears filled his eyes as he looked at the smoke words languishing and melting in the sky and bestowing upon him, in their inexhaustible charity and laughing goodness, one shape after another of unimaginable beauty and signalling their intention to provide him, for nothing, for ever, for looking merely, with beauty, more beauty! (p. 21)

His first thought, 'They are signalling to me', posits an agent, but then these words become free-floating in more than the literal sense, passing from potential signifiers ('He could not read the language yet') to independent signs, released – in Barthes's phrase – from bondage to the signified: 'he looked at the smoke words . . . bestowing upon him in their inexhaustible charity and laughing goodness, one shape after another of unimaginable beauty'.[8] The word for Woolf was not fixed, yet at the same time she felt strongly that language did have its own integrity.

The wealth of metaphors for language in Woolf's essays makes it clear that she regarded words as highly changeable, sometimes magical but often misleading. Yet the risk in unleasing language is taken because finally it can lead beyond itself. And here we come closer to the connection between language and reality, as Woolf saw it. In 'Hours in a Library' she speaks of how the new generation of writers 'will be casting their net out over some unknown abyss to snare new shapes, and we must throw our imaginations after them if we are to accept with understanding the strange gifts they bring back to us' (*CE* II, 39). Language is not fixed in its relation to the object, but it can generate a momentum, in spite of its inexactness, that can propel us to an apprehension of the object, which rests always in silence. Silence for Woolf was not menacing, though it was the zone of absence and death, it was also the realm of plenitude, meaning and presence. The task, as Woolf saw it, was not to articulate meaning, for that is ineffable, but to construct the arc of language which could take the reader there.

Norman Page argues that Woolf, aiming in *Mrs Dalloway* 'to catch the undirected and inconsequential quality of casual thought', avoids the traditional sentence with its 'hierarchical internal organization of main and subordinate clauses', eliminates co-ordinating or subordinating elements that we would normally expect, and provides instead sentences with a low degree of predictability, with features such as repetition, self-interruption and self-questioning that belong more obviously to spoken than to written prose and are designed to create the impression of a spontaneous flow of thought.[9] However, Page goes on, the haphazardness is more apparent than real, and her syntax exhibits a considerable degree of control. The prose is, in fact, heavily patterned, 'hardly less so than that of Gibbon or Pater', and possesses a rhythmic quality that places it 'closer to free verse than to the fictional prose of (say) H. G. Wells or Arnold Bennett' (p. 43).

Is Woolf trying to deceive us, attempting to reproduce the flow of spontaneous discourse, the sense of a speaking voice, but so imbued with Pater or Gibbon or Sir Thomas Browne that she cannot let go? Or are we meant to feel the pattern underneath? Not merely to recognise the discourse as stylised speech (in which case it is merely a convention that we decode and respond to accordingly) but to feel the contrary currents of speech and writing? She was always dissatisfied with the term 'novel' as a designation for her fiction, and she toyed with hybrid terms such as 'play-poem' – a term which embraces both speech and writing – for *The Waves*. I would suggest that the contradiction Page discerns was deliberate, and that she was consciously attempting to locate her discourse between speech and writing.

In the essay on *Twelfth Night* Woolf declares, 'The printed word is changed out of all recognition when it is heard by other people. . . . The word is given a body as well as a soul' (*CE* I, 29). Yet there is something lacking, for when Shakespeare 'wrote as a poet he was apt to write too quick for the human tongue. The prodigality of his metaphors can be flashed over by the eye, but the speaking voice falters in the middle' (*CE* I, 31). So we need something written. And yet she wants to preserve the qualities of the voice, qualities that have hitherto been the prerogative of poetry. Woolf speculates that in the novels yet to come there will be one 'written in prose, but in prose which has many characteristics of poetry. It will have something of the exaltation of poetry but much of the ordinariness of prose. It will be dramatic, and yet not a play. It will be read, not acted' (*CE* II, 224). Woolf's essays are notoriously about her own work; whether she is writing about Sterne, or Shakespeare, or Proust, however much she may illuminate her subject her commentary always reflects upon her craft. Clearly, in striving to invest her work with the qualities of orality she is seeking something more than spontaneity and casualness, something more profound than the stream of consciousness.

In fact, direct discourse is often absorbed in the voice of the narrator; where other novelists would present dialogue she reports it. She does not really have an ear for the language of the street (though it doesn't fail her when it is required), but her attention is directed elsewhere. In the manuscript of *Mrs Dalloway* there are long exchanges between Septimus and Bradshaw that are eliminated, and other conversations are subsumed by the narrative voice.[10] That voice comprehends a multitude of voices and diverse cadences, from casual conversation to formal apostrophe. It is true that the poetic rhythms of Woolf's prose disqualify it as 'truly spontaneous discourse', but Woolf is after something else. The rhythms are not the iambics of natural speech but the more structured rhythms of bardic recitation. In 'The Narrow Bridge of Art' she wonders, 'Can prose . . . chant the elegy, or hymn the love, or shriek in terror, or praise the rose, the nightingale, or the beauty of the night? . . . I think not. That is the penalty it pays for having dispensed with the incantation and the mystery' (*CE* II, 226). In *Mrs Dalloway* Woolf is trying to recover 'the incantation and the mystery'.

Woolf was not alone in her endeavours; hers were the central concerns of modernist literature. George Steiner, speaking of the 'crisis of poetic means' which began in the later nineteenth century,

notes that 'Rimbaud, Lautreamont, and Mallarmé strove to restore
to language a fluid, provisional character; they hoped to give back
to the word the power of incantation – of conjuring up the
unprecendented – which it possesses when it is still a form of
magic'.[11] Mallarmé, for instance, used words in 'occult and riddling
senses', making of them 'acts not primarily of *communication* but of
initiation into a private mystery' (p. 28). Woolf's innovations were
not so radical, but Steiner's distinctions are helpful for they
illuminate what Woolf was trying to do. She too was trying to
extend the possibilities of language, to make it fluid, but not to go
so far that it became provisional, riddling, occult. She hoped to
recapture the magical capabilities of language, and her works are
in a sense initiations into a mystery, but never at the expense of
communication; her vision is personal but not private.

At the end of the party we, with Peter, are initiated into the
mystery of Clarissa. Readers have doubted Clarissa's achievement,
claiming that it is 'more alleged than illustrated', or suggesting that
the communion, because evanescent, is 'spurious'; some wonder
whether the final statement is merely Peter's 'romantic affirmation
of a presence that sustains his melancholy', and charge that his
vision remains 'in the realm of assertion'.[12] Woolf herself regarded
Clarissa as 'tinselly' and perhaps not substantial enough to carry the
symbolic weight assigned to her (*D* III, 32).

In fact, the closing exchanges between Sally and Peter quite
deliberately cast doubt on the *raison d'être* of the party. Sally's
earnest belief that 'One must say simply what one felt', is deflated
by Peter's dubious rejoinder, '"But I do not know what I feel"' (p.
170). Sally concedes that she often despairs of human relationships, and seeks solace in her garden. She feels, she says, that
we are all prisoners scratching on the walls of our cells. But Peter
dissents; we *can* know one another he insists, and maintains that,
for his part, 'He did not like cabbages; he preferred human beings'
(p. 171). For the reader the explicit echo from the first page of the
novel, '"I prefer men to cauliflowers"' – Clarissa's remembrance of
Peter at Bourton – superimposes Peter upon his former self (in an
effect similar to Proust's closing party). The image is revealing.
Peter and Sally may not have solidified, as Clarissa feels her young
guests are certain to do, but they have not escaped a certain
hardening into habit. When Sally speaks with 'a rush of that
enthusiasm which Peter used to love her for', he finds it something
he 'dreaded a little now, so effusive she might become' (p. 169).

Her determination to say what one feels and Peter's preference for human beings now seem sentiments a little shopworn, stock responses rather than spontaneous affirmations of a personal creed. The effect is slightly grotesque; it is as if they age in an instant, frozen in poses struck thirty years ago at Bourton.

Habit insulates one from reality, from communion, and this is the condition Septimus avoids by refusing to compromise:

> They went on living ... they would grow old. A thing there was that mattered; a thing, wreathed about with chatter, defaced, obscured in her own life, let drop every day in corruption, lies, chatter. This he had preserved. Death was defiance. Death was an attempt to communicate, people feeling the impossibility of reaching the centre which, mystically, evaded them; closeness drew apart; rapture faded; one was alone. There was an embrace in death. (p. 163)

But if the moments of communion are never permanent, that does not deny their validity. They are inevitably grounded in time – Mrs Ramsay's successful dinner, crowned by Carmichael's invocation is, as they cross the threshold of the dining room, 'already the past'. There may be an embrace in death, but, to turn it around, the permanent embrace is death.

The temptation toward a state that transcends 'struggle and desire' is very strong for all of Woolf's characters. It is the realm Bernard longs to slide into once his dinner companion leaves: 'Let me cast and throw away this veil of being. ... Heaven be praised for solitude that has removed the pressure of the eye, the solicitation of the body, and all need of lies and phrases. ... How much better is silence' (W, 199). However, if the characters indulge a little in this temptation out of existence, it is always in order to more fully embrace life. Bernard returns to face death with defiance, and so too Clarissa returns, altered by Septimus's suicide. Through him she has achieved the contact with reality that has been eluding her at her own party. The change is conveyed to us through Peter. Earlier he had admired her abilities: 'Lolloping on the waves and braiding her tresses she seemed, having that gift still; to be; to exist; to sum it all up in the moment as she passed' (p. 154). Yet at this point Clarissa and Peter are still observers. Though she is pleased that Peter thinks her brilliant, she finds these 'triumphs' hollow. And for Peter she 'seems' to sum up; he sees the effects of her presence on the other guests, but he does not yet feel it. Now, as she returns having realised that love and the 'privacy of the soul' are not warring opposites but complementary aspects of the same impulse, she at last opens herself to life, and it is this that triggers Peter's vision: 'What is this terror? What is it that fills me with extraordinary excitement? It is Clarissa, he said. For there she was' (p. 172).

The first time Peter uses the phrase, 'there she was', it simply acknowledges his inability to describe Clarissa's effect upon others: 'Not that she was striking; not beautiful at all; there was nothing picturesque about her; she never said anything specially clever; there she was, however; there she was' (pp. 68–9). When it appears again it expresses all that she is and has become in her moment of fulfilment; she has at last become participant in, as well as architect of, her creation. Both she and Peter have resisted an opposing impulse, that temptation toward the more perfect, though inhuman, existence that Clarissa sees in the 'privacy of the soul' and Peter in the 'general peace' away from the 'fever of living', which the figure of nature offers in the dream of the solitary traveller. Thus the phrase also measures how far Peter has come, and further, it marks and embodies the reader's deepened engagement as well, for the *frisson* it evokes implicates us in his terror and excitement.

For we are moved; even readers who grant the ending only qualified success cannot deny its force. The general feeling seems to be that though we ought not to respond, we do. The reason has less to do with sentimentality than with language, specifically with the action of metaphor. As I have said, we feel the difference in emotional weight between the first time the phrase appears and its recurrence. This in itself is significant, but further, in registering the movement of the phrase from an expression of Peter's candid bafflement to the embodiment of his knowledge, full and precise if ineffable, of Clarissa, we acknowledge the transformation from cliché to metaphor. But as commentators on metaphor have pointed out, the reader in entering the figurative ground of a metaphor in order to grasp it is himself grasped or occupied.[13] This is what happens at the end of *Mrs Dalloway*: whether or not we choose upon reflection to credit the vision, in the act of reading we participate in it.

The event, like Mrs Ramsay's dinner party, dissolves in a moment and lasts forever. And the paradox it represents, in terms

of existence and of human consciousness, is also the paradox of
language. As Clarissa reflects on Septimus's suicide she wonders,
'But why had he done it? ... She had once thrown a shilling into
the Serpentine, never anything more. But he had flung it away' (p.
163). She reverses the meaning of 'it', and she does so again just
before she returns to the party: 'She felt glad that he had done it;
thrown it away while they went on living' (p. 165). Lucio Ruotolo
observes, 'Both life and death are bound indistinguishably in the
impersonal pronoun, one as obscure as the other; what has
Septimus lost and to what must Clarissa return?'[14] The confusion is
deliberate, the distinction employed and erased in the same breath.
It is a variation of the syntactical strategy used in the Regent's Park
scene, which immersed us in the up and down rhythm of the novel.
Life and death become interpenetrating, not just in theme and
dramatic action but in the dynamics of the prose. The effect is
accomplished here specifically through the shift in the implied
antecedent of the pronouns, but it is also achieved more generally
through the conjuction of speech and writing.

Speech is associated with life, presence, breath, but it is always
expiring, moving out of existence, towards silence. Writing, on the
other hand, is associated with death, deferral, fixity; it is silent
marks on a page; it belongs to that realm where all is unchanging,
ungrowing. Yet just as that zone of silence is, paradoxically, the
source of the characters' vitality and of their power to achieve
communion, so it is with writing. Miller argues that the action of
the novel is resurrected in the mind of the narrator, and that the
voice is from the first associated with the region of death, 'a place of
absence, where nothing exists but words'. However, 'these words
generate their own reality' (p. 199).

For Woolf the word is always striving toward orality, her novels
resolving themselves into cries at the edge of silence. The word
must be retrieved from writing in order to live. But, paradoxically,
it must first be written, has in a sense already been written.
However much the characters may resent its structures and its
strictures, language exists for them as writing, whether verbalised
or not. Their thinking is conditioned by literature – Clarissa lives
and feels through *Cymbeline* and *Othello*, Peter through attitudes
imbibed from Pope – but more important, even the incantatory
moan of the street singer depends for its full resonance on its
connection with a song by Richard Strauss and the tradition of All
Soul's Day.[15] There is always a trace. Woolf uses writing to direct us

toward speech, toward presence, toward origin, but with the knowledge that the movement is necessarily interrupted. Walter Benjamin speaks of the confrontation between 'signifying written language and intoxicating spoken language',[16] and Woolf, in 'A Sketch of the Past', distinguishes between language being used to create a 'concrete picture' and language being used to bring about a 'revelation of order' (*MB*, 122, 72). She does not take the further step that Benjamin does, but I think we can safely do so, and say that the vision comes finally not from language passing from the signifying to the intoxicating, from the concrete to the revelatory, but from the interplay between them.

Woolf's fictions are grounded in a world beyond the text, but they are meditations on the curious way in which that world exists only in the text. She does not resolve the issue but explores, dramatises, discusses, enacts the paradoxes of the relation in her work. Language moves out, from an initial connection with things, to pure pattern, to a connection with things once more, as the patterned artefact points beyond itself. Her endings are never conclusions, are always leaps into space rather than summations. The novels are gestures, in which we participate, toward a recovery/creation of presence, toward meaning inseparable from words and yet lying always just beyond language.

5
The Essays: The Subversive Process of Metaphor

Metaphor, for Virginia Woolf, was an instrument of inquiry as well as a means of crystallising an argument. In approaching a literary work she attempts, as Jane Novak says, 'to trace the artist's search, to produce an analysis of the effect',[1] and she does so by rendering her own search. But as in her novels, even as she leads us toward a particular insight, she alerts us to the controlling processes of language. In this chapter I am not going to be surveying the content of the essays. I want instead to examine their rhetorical strategies, drawing on the reading notes and the manuscript drafts, to show precisely how she engages the reader in her tracing of the artist's search.[2] More particularly, I shall be looking at the way she deploys her metaphors, at how they are used deliberately to disturb the reader's unquestioned assumptions, implicating him or her in Woolf's exploration of the complex relation between language, phenomenal reality and thought. Though I shall use other essays for examples, I have taken 'On Not Knowing Greek' as a paradigm, for it exhibits the qualities of both her critical reviews and her portraits.

Comparing Lamb and Hazlitt, Woolf notes that Lamb's method 'seems the flight of a butterfly cruising capriciously', while Hazlitt 'explores [the topic's] ramifications and scales its narrow paths as if it were a mountain road' (*CE* I, 159). Woolf herself often seems, perhaps, to be 'cruising capriciously' – indeed, she speaks of 'the flight of the mind' in connection with her essays – but in fact her metaphor for Hazlitt more closely captures her method. The image has the virtue of emphasising the patient labour which attends her progress (we have Leonard's testimony that she often rewrote a review seven times, and the extant drafts reveal much reworking), and it highlights the fact that the route is determined by the thing

67

itself and further that the intention is not to achieve a rigid straight-line progress, nor to cover all the ground. As she says in 'Coleridge as Critic', 'In literary criticism at least the wish to attain completeness is more often than not a will o' the wisp which lures one past the occasional ideas which may perhaps have truth in them towards an unreal symmetry which has none.'[3] In 'On Not Knowing Greek' it is apparent from the outset that she has no intention of achieving a rigid symmetry. She begins by asserting, 'It is obvious . . . the Greek literature is the impersonal literature', yet in the next paragraph she draws back, reassessing – 'But that is not . . . wholly true' – and then she sets off again, more tentatively, and with more attention to what is immediately at hand: 'Pick up any play by Sophocles, read – "Son of him who led our hosts at Troy of old, son of Agamemnon", and at once the mind begins to fashion itself surroundings' (*CE* I, 1). The apparent randomness and arbitrariness ('Pick up any play') resembles the beginning of the novels: where in *To the Lighthouse*, for example, she opens with a closely focused scene already in progress, here she chooses a line, not the first one, from a text and proceeds from there. And as in the novels one stage of the work succeeds another in a symmetry that is self-finding rather than imposed.

The paragraph structure supports this heuristic movement. Woolf will develop one line of argument without qualification and then without warning suddenly alter her position as she crosses the blank space between the paragraphs:

We have their poetry, and that is all.
But that is not . . . true.   (*CE* I, 1)

Almost half of the paragraphs in 'On Not Knowing Greek' begin with 'But', 'For' or 'Yet'. Pivoting on a disclaimer, Woolf leads and impels us on; actual changes in topic are likely to be effected with no moment of arrest somewhere in the middle of the paragraph. She uses her paragraphs almost as lines are used in verse: she may complete the thought within the paragraph, or, as in an enjambed line, the rhetorical unit may cut across the structural unit. Again, one finds the same thing in her novels, where she uses the paragraph divisions and occasionally even the chapter divisions to signal an emotional fluctuation rather then to mark a natural break in the action. In other words, the paragraphs chart the dips and turns of the flight of the mind rather than the formal stages of development in the argument.

The impetus of the essays derives in large part from the rhythm. It is that systolic/diastolic rhythm that takes many forms in the fiction – the absorption and withdrawal of Clarissa Dalloway, the smooth oscillations of the point of view in and out of characters' minds in *To the Lighthouse* – and in 'On Not Knowing Greek' there is a continuous movement from figure to ground and back again, as Woolf immerses the reader in the texture of a particular passage, moves out to consider the cultural context or further still to contrast Greek literature with the literature since that time, and then returns to a specific scene, fusing the whole in the narrative voice.

The technique can be unsettling. The narrative consciousness wanders out, unabashedly wool gathering, seemingly unconscious of direction; yet when we have almost forgotten the original subject we are returned to it with a snap. At the beginning of 'On Not Knowing Greek' Woolf sketches a scene of a crowded village and then moves on. The village seems to have been forgotten, but then, several pages later, she abruptly opens a paragraph with 'But winter fell on these villages' (*CE* I, 8). The reader is brought up short; the 'but' has nothing to do with the immediate antecedent, the dramatic language of the tragedians. Yet by taking us back to the beginning she forces the mind to loop around, enclosing the whole, and suddenly all the loosely connected remarks cohere: the chorus, character, the Greek language, all have been viewed against the backdrop of the village. She has not been digressing but taking us all around her subject, giving it an almost three-dimensional quality.

Much of what I have been suggesting about Woolf's method is consistent with Thomas Farrell's findings in 'The Female and Male Modes of Rhetoric'. He argues that the female mode of argument is one of 'indirection' which, unlike the male modes of induction and deduction, is characterised by its appearance of proceeding without a readily recognisable plan. The female mode, he says, comes closer to 'recreating the process of thinking', blurs the boundaries 'between the self of the author and the subject of the discourse, as well as between the self and the audience', and remains 'open-ended', all in contrast to the male modes of rhetoric. Farrell notes that Woolf uses both modes in *A Room of One's Own*, stating her thesis at the outset and repeating it several times toward the end (in the manner of the male mode of argument), but in the middle of the essay developing a 'train of thought' in the additive, open-ended mode of female rhetoric.[4] Woolf's essays are unique, but Farrell's conclusions highlight the extent to which she was working within, and helping to define, a recognisable mode of discourse. Further, at the end of his article Farrell offers the tentative conclusion that one must first master the male mode of rhetoric before attempting the female mode because the latter requires even greater control. Woolf's working papers demonstrate just how controlled her essays were, and they also show her working through the male mode in the preliminary stages, using it as a base for the free form of the finished work.

Woolf's essays give the impression of being still in process, a dialogue with the reader, and in fact she insisted that the best criticism was spoken (see 'Reviewing' or 'George Moore'). But reading through the manuscript volumes of reading notes and the early drafts of the essays one sees how painstaking her methods were, how carefully crafted the impression of artlessness. She succeeds, in large measure, because once launched on an article she did not revise so much as rewrite. In the five versions of 'Goldsmith', for instance, phrases and whole sentences will reappear intact but in a completely new context. Or material may shift from one essay to another, as with a paragraph on English humour which was carefully developed in the drafts of 'Notes on an Elizabethan Play' and then moved into 'On Not Knowing Greek' just before it was sent to the printers. In Woolf's essays there is less of the hardening into final form that one expects as a work jells. Rather, the material stays in solution and though there is a progressive refinement of the whole the various elements retain their capacity for recombination. Each draft, then, though in part a revision, is at the same time a beginning, and this freshness is sustained in the published essay. The ongoing creation within the process of revision is most marked at the level of figurative language. Almost all of the essays take shape around figures: Woolf will open with an image, which she then explores discursively, and then she will close with another, perhaps related, image which encapsulates the argument. One feels that these are the generative nodes of the essays, and in turning to the manuscript reading notes, the reader familiar with the diaries and letters might reasonably expect to find brilliant *aperçus*, cast in the form of similes or metaphors, out of which the filaments of discursive thought will unravel for the finished article. Surprisingly, though, the images around which the argument crystallises most often come in at a later stage of composition, after she has blocked out the argument. It is only after she has taken a theme as far as she can with discursive prose that she moves to an image, completing the analytic in the poetic mode. Her remarks on Proust in 'Phases of Fiction' describe her own method:

> As a consequence of the union of the thinker and the poet, often, on the heel of some fanatically precise observation, we come upon a flight of imagery – beautiful, coloured, visual, as if the mind, having carried its powers as far as possible in analysis, suddenly rose in the air and from a station high up gave us a different view of the same object in terms of metaphor.
>
> (*CE* II, 85)

The metaphors may come last in the stages of composition, but they are the reverse of decorative. They are the natural outgrowth of a prose that is radically – though not at all obviously – metaphoric.

Describing Ellen Terry's voice, Woolf says, 'It was as if someone drew a bow over a ripe, richly seasoned, cello; it grated, it glowed, and it growled' (*CE* IV, 67). What is interesting here is not the simile but the verbs that elaborate it. It is these characteristic strings of verb metaphors which most clearly illustrate Woolf's conceptions of language and reality, and the following passage from 'On Not Knowing Greek' reveals how her metaphors which decline to specify a tenor express her sense of the complex and problematic relation between the world and the word. The passage is the culmination of her discussion of Plato, her paean to his 'dramatic genius'. I have italicised the verbs:

> For Plato, of course, had the dramatic genius. It is by means of that, by an art which conveys in a sentence or two the setting and the atmosphere, and then with perfect adroitness *insinuates* itself into the coils of the argument without losing its liveliness and grace, and then *contracts* to bare statement, and then, *mounting*, *expands* and *soars* in that higher air which is generally reached only by the more extreme measures of poetry – it is this art which plays upon us in so many ways at once and brings us to an exultation of mind which can only be reached when all the powers are called upon to contribute their energy to the whole. (*CE* I, 9–10)

The dialogues engage the reader completely in the search for truth, 'for', she says, 'Plato had the dramatic genius'. We now expect Woolf to elaborate, to define 'dramatic genius'. She does so, but not in the conventional manner. This 'genius' is an 'art' which concisely 'conveys . . . the setting and the atmosphere'. Thus far we are on firm ground. This art, however, then 'insinuates' itself into the coils of the argument, and it does so 'with perfect adriotness' and 'without losing its liveliness and grace'. The action and the qualities imply something animate or possibly even human, though there is no indication of what specifically is to be imagined. Yet in the next phrase it 'contracts' to bare statement and then, 'mounting', it 'expands and soars'. The implied noun is now certainly not something human, and it seems to be passing out of the realm of the animate, able as it is to 'contract' then 'expand' as it 'soars'. Do we then move from a conduit, a hose, say, to a snake ('coils' prompts that association), to a bird to a hot air balloon or a bubble, before it (the art, remember) becomes perhaps a sun – for finally it 'plays upon us'? The suggestions are absurd, and I introduce them to emphasise what Woolf's figures do not do and to highlight the distinction between noun metaphors and verb metaphors.

Christine Brooke-Rose argues that the chief difference between the two types is one of explicitness: 'With the noun, A is called B, more or less clearly according to the link. But the verb changes one noun into another by implication.'[5] Because the change is only implied,

> although the metaphoric verb does in a sense 'replace' the action more normally associated with the stated noun, we do not have to be aware of that replacement, as we do with the noun metaphor. . . . In Geoffrey of Vinsauf's example, 'the meadows *laugh*', *laugh* does of course replace 'are gay with flowers', or, more literally still, 'are full of flowers'. But we do not have to make this translation consciously. . . . The picture of the meadows laughing is immediate, and 'Meadows' are indirectly humanized, but indirectly enough not to be ridiculous.
>
> (pp. 207–8)

Finally, and for our purposes the most important point, because the change in the noun is implicit rather than explicit, 'the change can be much less decisive: the noun can become one of many things' (p. 212). In Woolf's series the verbs are consistent even if the nouns are not; that does not trouble us. In any case, the passage develops in a chain reaction, with one image touching off another so quickly that one has no time to visualise them. The passage does not merely move quickly, carried swiftly in parallel phrases – 'conveys . . . and then . . . insinuates . . . and then contracts . . . and then, mounting, expands and soars', it accelerates. Not only do the phrases become shorter; in the second phrase the verb moves closer to the preposition and the adverbs are jettisoned as the passage begins to take off, and by the third series the verbs, now a series within the series, lose their modifiers as the implied noun soars free of the earth and, incidentally, of the substantive level which the reader, at the beginning, might have been trying to hold it to. Finally, with the reiteration of the subject ('it is this art which plays') the implied noun rests serene, invested with properties that make it particular, palpable and animate – certainly possessed of its own impetus – yet impossible to visualise. Unlike a single verb metaphor, such as 'time flaps on the mast' (*MD*, 45), where the implied noun, a sail in light winds, is easily visualised, here there is nothing so specific for the mind to cling to. While there is consistency among the nouns, they do not neatly cohere. In her treatment of Plato's art, the quasi-human, the animate and the inanimate all lend different qualities to the abstraction.

The examples above illustrate another distinctive characteristic of Woolf's images: their vaguely disturbing quality. Irma Ranta-vaara in her study of *The Waves* speaks of the 'bold metaphors, unusual combinations and juxtapositions, together with the frequent use of antithesis' that constitute Woolf's 'shock technique'.[6] Metaphor is by definition unsettling, effecting as it does a transfer from one realm to another, and from Aristotle onward there is a feeling that this transfer is not quite proper. A more extreme instance of this, the 'application of a term to a thing it does not properly denote' is catachresis: the deliberate 'misuse' of words.[7] The figure has a legitimate function, yet as Paul de Man says, 'Something monstrous lurks in the most innocent of catachreses: when one speaks of the legs of the table or the face of the mountain, catachresis is already turning into prosopopeia, and one begins to perceive a world of potential ghosts and monsters.' Catachresis can 'dismember the texture of reality and reassemble it in the most capricious of ways'.[8] Something of this obtains in Woolf's series of images. The implied nouns do not demand to be visualised, and we grant that the concept under consideration is being viewed from different angles. Yet there is still a hint of something monstrous which we cannot dispel.

I have said that we do not visualise these figures, but there is none the less a half-formed impression, a vague retinal image, that attends them. This 'capriciousness' and the hint of something unnatural is consistent with the view of life one finds in the novels, where something monstrous seems to lurk beneath the placid surface of everyday reality – the chaos outside the dinner table in *To the Lighthouse* or that realm without change or love 'where the eyeless wind blows', which Isa drifts into in *Between the Acts* – and it will occasionally break through in the language of the essays. This tendency toward catechresis and the world view implied by it is, of course, but an extension of a view of life that is essentially metaphoric. 'Now is life very shifting or very solid?' she asks in the *Diary* (III, 218), and metaphor captures this irreconcilable conjunction of 'is' and 'is not'. Metaphor is for Woolf the most appropriate instrument for exploring, or participating in, reality. Paul Ricoeur, in examining the link between the heuristic function and the descriptive function in metaphor argues that metaphor represents the conjunction of poiesis and mimesis.[9] He insists on the fusion of the creative and the referential in metaphor. I would like to go further and suggest that for Woolf this relation obtained in language as a whole; for any writer the descriptive and the poetic functions of language are not ultimately separable, but for Woolf they were practically indistinguishable. She scorned the Victorians who in their poetry attempted to number the steaks of the tulip; what she was after, even in dealing with phenomenal reality, was something much more elusive, and thus no description, however prosaic, is free of the poetic element. And neither is any analysis.

Ricoeur addresses the question of whether or not there is an 'ordinary' language within which metaphor works, an opposition between 'proper' and 'figurative'. For Woolf there was not, but that does not mean she was not conscious of transgressing boundaries. Her figure, 'the far side of language', suggests a boundary or a barrier, and in her essays she attempts to do what she describes Aeschylus as doing, to launch the reader toward a meaning beyond language. Further, she is quite consciously extending the frontier, for if she is successful, the meaning, heretofore inaccessible to language, will now have been brought (both created and described) within its province. In addition to whatever immediate purpose she may have, this extending of language is always her larger aim, and it is as strong an impulse in the essays as it is in the novels.

Her technique involved obvious risks, and the possibility of falling into a fatal looseness did concern her. In the diary entry for 23 June 1929 she writes,

> At Rodmell I read through the Common Reader; & this is very important – I must learn to write more succinctly. Especially in the general idea essays like the last, How it strikes a Contemporary, I am horrified by my own looseness. This is partly that I don't think things out first; partly that I stretch my style to take in crumbs of meaning. But the result is a wobble & diffusity & breathlessness which I detest.   (*D* III, 235)

Her charges may at times seem justified (though her severe appraisal probably had as much to do with the fact that she was correcting *A Room of One's Own* – 'And so I am pitched into my great lake of melancholy' – as with the style of the essays) but the fact is that this breathlessness was carefully orchestrated. A dramatic example of her controlled pacing appears at the opening of her essay on Coleridge, 'The Man at the Gate'. She utters his name and it opens a floodgate:

> The Man was Coleridge as De Quincey saw him, standing in a gateway. For it is vain to put the single word Coleridge at the head of a page – Coleridge the innumerable, the mutable, the atmospheric; Coleridge who is part of Wordsworth, Keats, and Shelley; of his age and of our own; Coleridge whose written words fill hundreds of pages and overflow innumerable margins; whose spoken words still reverberate, so that as we enter his radius he seems not a man, but a swarm, a cloud, a buzz of words, darting this way and that, clustering, quivering, and hanging suspended.

Then she stops herself, 'it is well before we become dazed in the labyrinth of what we call Coleridge to have a clear picture before us'. She quotes De Quincey, and then she proceeds soberly. The sentences become short, declarative, matter-of-fact:

> That was in 1807. Coleridge was already incapable of movement. The Kendal black drop had robbed him of his will. . . . The arms already hung flabby at his side; he was powerless to raise them.   (*CE* III, 217)

I wish to emphasise that Woolf's stylistic flights are never gratuitous, and, paradoxical as it may sound, that they are always firmly anchored. In 'Notes on an Elizabethan Play' she speaks of how the Elizabethans bore us because they 'soar miles into the empyrean', giving us nothing but a cloud landscape, where the sensibility of the modern reader requires that literature 'have one toe touching Liverpool' (*CE* I, 55). Stylistically, Woolf always has that toe touching Liverpool; a firm syntactic structure (however idiosyncratic her use of the semicolon) and a fondness for antithesis prevail no matter how many items she may pile up in a series or how many series she may string together in a given passage. Just as in the novels she explores the ebb and flow of consciousness without departing from conventional syntax, so in the essays she soars and loops, but the vehicle for this flight remains a carefully shaped sentence. In her prodigality of language we see her affinity with the Elizabethan prose writers such as Thomas Browne and Dekker whom she so admired: 'I bathed myself in Dekker last night', she writes in her diary, 'as in my natural element' (*D* IV, 42). Yet in her control she recalls the eighteenth-century essayists.

The idea of 'stretching' a style, as if it were something palpable and elastic – an 'envelope', perhaps, to use one of her favourite metaphors for style – suggests that meaning is something separate that is contained in the words. The implications of Woolf's metaphors for language are important especially because Woolf herself insists on the close relation between the perception of phenomenal reality and language. In 'A Sketch of the Past' she says that when she receives a sudden 'shock' of perception, 'it is or will become a revelation of some order; it is a token of some real thing behind appearance; and I make it real by putting it into words. It is only by putting it into words that I make it whole' (*MB*, 72). The controlling figure in this passage, putting the revelation '*into*' words, is an instance of what Michael J. Reddy calls the 'conduit' metaphor, the metaphor which in its various forms (Reddy lists 140) determines the way in which we conceive of language.[10] The problem is that what is actually transmitted is not a 'message' but signals, a 'blueprint' from which the bearer reconstructs the message. This may seem obvious enough, but too often we speak as if message and signal were identical, and that implies that success in communication is automatic. If we 'decant' meaning into words, to use another of Woolf's metaphors, then presumably all the reader has to do is to pour out the meaning in order to understand. But if we think in terms of sending blueprints rather than the thing itself we will not expect the communication to be flawless; partial communication, multiple readings of a single text, become the norm rather than errors requiring explanation. However, though it is easy enough to acknowledge this, we are trapped by the very phrases we use to describe language. They appear neutral but they are not, and it is difficult to get outside them (I say, using a conduit metaphor) in order to look at language itself. They are metaphors we use mindlessly, channelling our thought without stimulating it to the point where we become conscious of the process.

Yet 'decant', to return to the Woolf's expression, differs in that there is still a fairly high degree of metaphorical activity in the image; it has not become lexicalised (as, say, 'put meaning *into* words' has) and it is used deliberately. And this is a comparatively mild example. What is remarkable in Woolf's essays is the extent to which language is given metaphorical form. Words may become a rocket, a cloud, a net, a veil, a glove, an envelope, or some other concrete but undefined thing; they may become animated as a bird, an insect, a fish, a lizard, a beast of burden, or some other living but unspecified form; they may become personified in a number of ways, from a 'horde of rebels' to a shapely goddess. While Reddy contends that 'becoming cognizant' of our habitual assumptions does not alter the situation, Woolf's art is founded on the assumption that becoming cognizant can help, that in fact it is vital.

In all of her novels the characters struggle with language. One thinks immediately of Bernard in *The Waves* or Miss La Trobe in *Between the Acts*, but beginning with Rachel, the heroine of *The Voyage Out*, these grapplings with the concepts of personal identity and of reality are grounded in or at least inseparable from the characters' questionings about the functions of language. In Woolf's essays one discovers the same restlessness as in the novels. There is delight but also dissatisfaction in her playing with words. She is determined to make discourse visible, not simply by the high degree of imagery in her prose but by constantly challenging the reader's notion of language, forcing him or her to think of it as something palpable, but also protean, something that has not only integrity but independence, something at times capricious, even untrustworthy, perhaps perverse.

The fact that the essays are addressed to a common reader – however idealised the conception of that reader may be – is important. Woolf is conscious of the difficulty of communication,

knows that it can be effected only by great effort, and thus provides
a shower of images, in part to capture the complexity of the thing
under consideration, but also to provide a number of possible
points of connection, a number of blueprints we might say, except
that one need only apprehend one image fully for the others then
to become instantly intelligible as well. Further, these metaphors
create a more receptive condition in the audience, nudging or
jolting readers out of their complacency about language and their
assuredness that there is a fixed relation between language and
reality, and that they can effortlessly extract the meaning; the
figures enlist the reader as an active partner in this delicate and
difficult business of communication. Whatever her subject, Woolf's
rhetorical intent in every aspect of the essay from the structure of
the paragraphs to the design of the metaphors is the same: to
subvert the conceptual strictures of language, to liberate the author
and the reader from what Nietzsche called 'the prison-house of
language'.

6

To the Lighthouse: From Social Language to Incantation

The title *To the Lighthouse* indicates a voyage, but as so often in modernist literature it is a psychic voyage. The novel is dominated by process – life to death, youth to maturity, promise to fulfilment both in the completion of a work of art and in the movement beyond the individual self to contact with some larger reality – but it is the process of living and 'the flight of the mind', rather than the external events, that concern Woolf. As it renders this flight, the book also explores the submerged aspects of language, dramatising the workings of social chat and poetic chant, as well as unvoiced meditation, and at the same time working silently on the reader. Here meaning is more often conveyed by syntax than denotation, by echo than by exposition, in a prose that more than any of her novels fulfils her criteria for the 'feminine sentence'.

It is Lily who most strongly challenges the position expressed by Clarissa Dalloway, who extolled 'the enormous resources of the English language, the power it bestows, after all, of communicating feelings' (*MD*, 195). Late in the book, when Lily's sense of loss has become almost excruciating, she wants to speak to Carmichael but finds she cannot express her anguish:

> she wanted to say not one thing, but everything. Little words that broke up the thought and dismembered it said nothing. 'About life, about death; about Mrs Ramsay' – no, she thought, one could say nothing to nobody. The urgency of the moment always missed its mark. Words fluttered sideways and struck the object inches too low. . . . For how could one express in words these emotions of the body? (p. 165)

The narrator of *Jacob's Room* had complained that 'Even the exact words get the wrong accent on them' (*JR*, 72); here no such exactness is predicated.

Yet as the exchange between the Ramsays at the end of Part I suggests, words cannot on that account be dispensed with. The strain between Mr and Mrs Ramsay, occasioned by their disagreement over the weather, continues unresolved until the end of the day; and during dinner Mrs Ramsay longs for even 'one word', reflecting that, 'It was altogether different when he spoke; one did not feel then, pray heaven you don't see how little I care, because one did care' (pp. 88–9). Later, as they sit reading, she needs to hear his voice: 'For the shadow, the thing folding them in was beginning, she felt, to close round her again. Say anything, she begged' (p. 113). At last he speaks, '"You won't finish that stocking to-night," he said, pointing to her stocking. That was what she wanted – the asperity in his voice reproving her. If he says it's wrong to be pessimistic probably it is wrong' (p. 113). For her part, Mrs Ramsay cannot give him the explicit declaration of love he requires. However, she consolidates their love and resolves the morning's dispute: '"Yes, you were right. It's going to be wet to-morrow." She had not said it, but he knew it. And she looked at him smiling. For she had triumphed again' (p. 114).[1] Most of the complicated give-and-take of this scene occurs in silence, yet it has been necessary for the communication to surface in language in order to bring about the final reconciliation.

It appears that if one does not demand too much of words, using them to approach the matter of importance obliquely, they will communicate one's emotions. In the passages quoted above the semantic content of the utterance is of some importance, but in each case the speech functions primarily as a signal, a sign of affirmation. The characters are making use of a slightly more intimate version of the special language Mrs Ramsay employs to overcome the separateness at the beginning of the dinner. She inquires of Bankes, 'Did you find your letters?' (p. 79). Bankes replies, and in turn observes, 'It's odd that one scarcely gets anything worth having by post, yet one always wants one's letters' (p. 80). Tansley regards these pleasantries as 'damned rot'. But, the narrator explains, they are part of a 'social' language:

> So, when there is a strife of tongues at some meeting, the
> chairman, to obtain unity, suggests that every one shall speak

French. Perhaps it is bad French; French may not contain the words that express the speaker's thoughts; nevertheless speaking French imposes some order, some uniformity.... and Mr Tansley, who had no knowledge of this language, even spoken thus in words of one syllable, at once suspected its sincerity. (p. 84)

Just as he could not appreciate the importance of getting letters that seldom contain 'anything worth having', so he cannot see that these social expressions, devoid of literal import, have demonstrable value as gestures.

Language does have 'enormous resources', though not perhaps of the kind Clarissa Dalloway supposed. To return to Lily, at one point early in the book she considers the character of Mr Ramsay, wondering how one can judge people, 'and conclude that it was liking one felt, or disliking? And to those words what meaning attached after all?' (p. 27). The narrow precision of words causes them to distort. At this same moment, however, she is standing 'transfixed' beside the pear tree with impressions pouring in upon her:

and to follow her thought was like following a voice which speaks too quickly to be taken down by one's pencil, and the voice was her own voice saying without prompting undeniable everlasting, contradictory things.   (p. 27)

The passage (which is strikingly similar to Woolf's account of her compositional process in 'A Sketch of the Past') indicates that language, when it is restored to its poetic or metaphorical nature, can successfully embody experience. But in doing so it must transcend logic: these utterances are at once 'undeniable', 'everlasting' and 'contradictory'.

Language comes unbidden to Mrs Ramsay as well, as she gazes at the lighthouse, descending into her 'wedge of darkness'. In this scene words become part of the process of losing the self, acting like a mantra to empty the mind and make it receptive to non-conceptual experience. Mrs Ramsay feels the need 'to think; well not even to think. To be silent; to be alone' (p. 60). Then the rhythm of the light calls forth a phrase: 'Often she found herself sitting and looking ... until she became the thing she looked at – that light for example. And it would lift up on it some little phrase or other ... which she would repeat and begin adding to' (p. 61).

Although the process is not foolproof (an unbidden reference to the Lord momentarily jars her), this stage of half-deliberate meditation prepares her for her ecstatic union with the lighthouse beam. Her experience differs from the dinner guests' in that the words themselves do not seem to contain truth, yet in both cases the rhythm of the language helps effect the transition from the analytical to the contemplative mode of perception, readying the mind for a moment of non-rational insight.

As so often in this novel, poetic effect anticipates exposition. Before we are told of the words washing rhythmically in Mrs Ramsay's mind, the author's rhythms begin to wash through our own: 'now a weed, now a straw, now a bubble, . . . sinking deeper . . . she fell deeper and deeper' (p. 109). And earlier, before she mentions the little phrases that lift up from the floor of Mrs Ramsay's mind, Woolf conveys the hypnotic quality of a repeated word or phrase through the account of Mrs Ramsay's merging with the beam.

> and pausing there she looked out to meet that stroke of the Lighthouse, the long steady stroke, for watching them in this mood always at this hour one could not help attaching oneself to one thing especially of the things one saw; and this thing, the long steady stroke, was her stroke.   (p. 61)

The repetition of 'one could . . . oneself . . . one thing . . . things one saw', and more particularly of 'stroke . . . long steady stroke . . . long steady stroke . . . stroke', sets up a litany of the sort that comes to Mrs Ramsay. Thus we apprehend more fully the quality specified in the subsequent description. In her own narration, as in the dramatic action, Woolf explores the incantatory power of language.

Later in the evening, Mrs Ramsay's chant operates in a similar fashion. In the course of the dinner the guests have progressed from the anarchy of truculent silences and veiled jibes, through the willed cordiality of social language, to a harmony which, Mrs Ramsay feels, partakes of the eternal. Finally, that harmony (which is beyond language) is articulated in the chant. Whereas the fragments of poetry Mr Ramsay has been declaiming throughout the day have served as the index of his private emotions, now the verse expresses the feelings of the group. Mrs Ramsay does 'not know what they meant, but, like music, the words seemed to be . . .

saying quite easily and naturally what had been in her mind the whole evening while she said different things' (p. 102). So too for the guests, the words sound 'as if no one had said them' and at the same time as if 'this were, at last, the natural thing to say, this were their own voice speaking' (p. 102). The sense of the voice as both disembodied and personal recalls Lily's experience under the pear tree, as does the fact that the words, while resisting intellectual interpretation, effortlessly and exactly give shape to their emotions.

After dinner when Mrs Ramsay reads the sonnet, she does so in the same way that she approaches the lighthouse beam. Leafing through her anthology she feels that she is 'climbing backwards, upwards, shoving her way up under petals that curved over her, so that she only knew this is white or this is red. She did not know at first what the words meant at all' (p. 110). She begins to merge with the poetry, and the images chart her descent: the words, at first like lights within her mind, become a landscape into which she moves. Mr Ramsay, meanwhile, reads a Walter Scott novel with enthusiasm. It takes him away from his own concerns, crystallizing and discharging the exaltation and melancholy he had felt earlier: he 'forgot his bothers and failures completely in poor Steenie's drowning and Mucklebackit's sorrow (that was Scott at his best) now and the astonishing delight and feeling of vigour that it gave him' (pp. 110–11). Although he responds to the emotion embodied in the work, he maintains a certain detachment: 'But he must read it again. He could not remember the whole shape of the thing. He had to keep his judgement in suspense' (p. 111).

In contrast to her husband, Mrs Ramsay's engagement with the Shakespeare sonnet is unqualified:

> All the odds and ends of the day stuck to this magnet; her mind felt swept, felt clean. And then there it was, suddenly entire shaped in her hands, beautiful and reasonable, clear and complete, the essence sucked out of life and held rounded here – the sonnet. (p. 111)

Mr Ramsay wonders 'if she understood what she was reading. Probably not, he thought' (p. 112). The glib rhyme of his dismissal, while characterising Mr Ramsay, reminds the reader that a different order of understanding has taken place.

These passages in 'The Window' that deal with language form a progression. Lily's experience under the pear tree hints at the realising potential of language. Mrs Ramsay's descent into a wedge of darkness reveals the incantatory power of language. Mr Ramsay's chant displays both qualities, although in a comparatively superficial manner. The rhythm of the verse does not produce a state of absorption as intense as that of Mrs Ramsay's reverie; and the actual words, speaking as they do of things exalted and melancholy, help to focus the emotions of the guests, but certainly do not yield the essence of life. The reading scene exposes the triviality of the supper table verse; Woolf lets it serve simply as incantation, and presents in the sonnet the full exploitation of that power Lily had discovered in her vision by the tree.

We began this discussion with Lily's silent wail, 'How could one express in words these emotions of the body? express that emptiness there?' (p. 165), observing that although a 'social' language is necessary and useful in the exchange of emotions, only when language becomes 'poetic' can it express such things as Lily's desolation. And in fact, the next moment, in answer to her silent question to Carmichael – 'What does it all mean? How do you explain it all?' (p. 166) – Lily suddenly feels, 'That would have been his answer, presumably – how "you" and "I" and "she" pass and vanish; nothing stays; all changes; but not words, not paint' (p. 166). Finally, one cannot 'explain', for denotative prose 'dismembers'; but lasting truths can be apprehended and communicated through the experience of art.

In her own work of art, Woolf wishes to guide the reader to the perception of the elementary but complex truth that, as James discovers, 'Nothing was simply one thing' (p. 172). To do so her novel must not just sensitively describe, but like the sonnet, capture the 'essence of life'. Lily's thoughts (most readers have noted that she thinks of her painting in literary terms) provide an accurate statement of Woolf's position: 'Phrases came. Visions came. . . . But what she wished to get hold of was that very jar on the nerves, the thing itself before it has been made anything' (p. 178). To catch that undifferentiated 'thing itself' one must unite both the analytical and the intuitive perspectives of reality. As Lily observes, 'All that in idea seemed simple became in practice immediately complex; as the waves shape themselves symmetrically from the cliff top, but to the swimmer among them are divided by steep gulfs, and foaming crests' (p. 147). And in the course of reading, Woolf's audience learns to reconcile intense immersion in experience with cliff-top detachment.

The three large blocks of narration are dominated respectively
by Mrs Ramsay's intuition, Mr Ramsay's empiricism, and Lily's
fusion of the two. Woolf presents these perspectives discursively,
through the thoughts and conversations of the characters. More
importantly, she incorporates them in the prose, so that in reading
we experience the given mode of perception, often shifting within
a single sentence from one character to another, though still
controlled by a narrator; for example, on the second page of the
book, James's reaction to his father's curt dismissal of the projected
voyage. He despises his father who stands by the window,

> grinning sarcastically . . . casting ridicule upon his wife, who was
> ten thousand times better in every way than he was (James
> thought), but also with some secret conceit at his own accuracy of
> judgement. (p. 10)

'Ten thousand times better' is obviously James's idiom, but 'secret
conceit' returns us to the narrator. The passage then segues into
Mrs Ramsay's idiom:

> He was incapable of untruth; never tampered with a fact; never
> altered a disagreeable word to suit the pleasure or convenience
> of any mortal being, least of all his children who,

(here we move to Mr Ramsay's mode)

> should be aware from childhood that life is difficult; facts
> uncompromising; and the passage to that fabled land where our
> brightest hopes are extinguished,

(and now the thought swerves inevitably toward the black hole of
his ego)

> our frail barks founder in darkness (here Mr Ramsay would
> straighten his back and narrow his little blue eyes upon the
> horizon), one that needs, above all, courage, truth, and the
> power to endure.

The passage begins with James's caustic criticism, passes through
Mrs Ramsay's resentful dissent and ends in Mr Ramsay's self-
pitying melodrama. The drama, the central conflict around which
the book takes shape, develops from the three minds contending,

but it is a contest that takes place silently; James doesn't speak at all
and Mrs Ramsay replies mildly, 'But it may be fine – I expect it will
be fine.' The indirect interior monologue allows Woolf to render
the nuances of this submerged struggle.

Yet the narrator's role is not innocent. As the reader discovers in
Part III, she is here shaping our response to Mr Ramsay, leading us
to regard him with mockery so that later she can force us to reassess
him – and question our own judgement in the process. While
reflecting upon Mr Ramsay's study of 'subject and object and the
nature of reality', Lily recalls Andrew's helpful advice: '"Think of a
kitchen table . . . when you're not there"', and thus she muses,

> Naturally, if one's days were passed in this seeing of angular
> essences, this reducing of lovely evenings, with all their flamingo
> clouds and blue and silver to a white deal four-legged table (and
> it was a mark of the finest minds to do so), naturally one could
> not be judged like an ordinary person.   (p. 26)

Not only does the sentence expertly express the gap between an
empirical and a contemplative perspective, it subtly enlists our
support for the latter. The phrase 'passed in this seeing of angular
essences' is itself awkward and angular: the words resist elision, and
the sibilants demand precise articulation. On the other hand, Lily's
vision of 'lovely evenings, with all their flamingo clouds and blue
and silver' flows easily, and we suddenly have colour, and a touch
of extravagance with 'flamingo'. All of which contrasts dramatically
with the no-nonsense enumeration of particulars that follows: 'a
white deal four-legged table'. The passage is more than exposition,
for the language embodies what it indicates.

At this point neither Lily nor the reader is free of Mrs Ramsay's
perspective. In 'Time Passes', however, fact rather than intuition
dominates, as fine aesthetic discriminations are lost in the natural
chaos. There the description of another lovely evening is abruptly
punctured by the interpolated announcement of Prue's death:

> [Prue Ramsay died that summer in some illness connected with
> childbirth, which was indeed a tragedy, people said. They said
> nobody deserved happiness more.]   (p.123)

The tone, even more than the brackets, enforces our detachment.
Prue's death is 'a tragedy, people said': the brief qualifier dissoci-

ates us from the event. And without human meditation to enhance the significance of the occasion (for we are now in the domain of chronological rather than subjective time) her death and those of Andrew and Mrs Ramsay must be viewed as minor occurrences in the cosmic whirl. The phenomenal reality, not the human impression of it, claims our attention. From our present standpoint, it is the enthusiasm for 'flamingo clouds', not the dogged analysis of the plain table, that would seem ludicrous.

Our experience of time passing corresponds to Lily's, for in 'The Lighthouse' she looks upon Mr Ramsay's quest with new respect:

> The kitchen table was something visionary, austere; something bare, not hard, not ornamental. . . . But Mr Ramsay kept always his eyes fixed upon it . . . until his face became worn too and ascetic and partook of this unornamented beauty which so deeply impressed her.   (pp. 145–6)

'Visionary' and 'austere' convey a sense of something admirable, in contrast to the slightly sardonic earlier characterisation of his work as the 'seeing of angular essences'. She has learned that she must include the intellectual toughness of Mr Ramsay's vision in her art, as Woolf indicates through Lily's description of her projected painting:

> Beautiful and bright it should be on the surface, feathery and evanescent, one colour melting into another like the colours on a butterfly's wing; but beneath the fabric must be clamped together with bolts of iron.   (p. 159)

The apprehension of delicate beauty now takes shape upon an unblinking regard for facts.

The reader, too, participates in this more encompassing perspective. For example, as the boat approaches the lighthouse the narrator observes,

> One could hear . . . the waves rolling and gambolling and slapping the rocks as if they were wild creatures who were perfectly free and tossed and tumbled and sported like this for ever.   (p. 190)

Although the picture is one of playful innocence it sustains an ominous undercurrent, for the passage echoes the account in 'Time Passes' of a horrendous 'chaos ... tumbling and tossing, as the wind and waves disported themselves like the amorphous bulk of leviathans ... in idiot games' (p. 125). Thus the cross-references that tie the book together (the 'bolts of iron') conspire to lead the reader to a full apprehension of the contradictory nature of life. During the dinner Lily is struck by the 'complexity of things', and she notes that the Ramsays make her 'feel violently two opposite things at the same time' (p. 95). Woolf does the same thing to her audience; and it is in that clash of opposites that we may momentarily glimpse 'the thing itself before it has been made anything'.

The conjuction of opposites occurs most strikingly in the figure of Mrs Ramsay, who appears to the reader and to the other characters as both a symbol and as an ordinary human being. Lily ponders the 'spirit', 'the essential thing' in Mrs Ramsay:

> Was it wisdom? Was it knowledge? Was it, once more the deceptiveness of beauty ... or did she lock up within her some secret which certainly Lily Briscoe believed people must have for the world to go on at all?   (p. 50)

For Bankes it is a force that can harmonise the elements; for Lily it is the key to harmony in the human sphere. In the dinner scene Woolf dramatises the action of this potent inner 'spirit'.

With her social language and her personal abilities as a hostess, Mrs Ramsay brings everyone to a common level of cordiality. Then, with the lighting of the candles, 'Some change at once went through them all ... and they were all conscious of making a party together in a hollow, on an island; had their common cause against that fluidity out there' (p. 91). The situation has now been resolved into a conflict between Mrs Ramsay and her perennial enemy, the disorder of 'life'. She responds to the challenge, and the reader begins to feel the workings of her harmonising power.

Her weapon against chaos is marriage. We have already been told that her influence has precipitated Paul's proposal to Minta, and at this moment, as the guests join in league against the fluidity outside, the young couple enters. Woolf's presentation of the scene enforces our sense of Mrs Ramsay's authority:

> anything might happen Lily felt. They must come now, Mrs Ramsay thought, looking at the door, and at that instant, Minta

Doyle, Paul Rayley, and a maid carrying a great dish in her hands
came in together.   (p. 91)

'They must come now', carries the certainty of fiat, as well as the
hopefulness of prediction. Mrs Ramsay's thought, the entrance of
the couple, and the arrival of the Boeuf en Daube (focus and
emblem of the group communion) all coincide. The tableau and
the syntactical strategy used to present it make the moment
arresting, yet fully integrated with the narrative. There are no
rhetorical signposts urging us to take notice, yet we do not fail to
decide – by ourselves, it seems – that the moment is significant, and
that it somehow testifies to Mrs Ramsay's extraordinary nature.
When the moment of harmony occurs it is specifically her
moment, which also embraces them all:

> she hovered like a hawk suspended; like a flag floated in an
> element of joy . . . [which] seemed now for no special reason to
> stay there like a smoke, like a fume rising upwards, holding them
> safe together. Nothing need be said; nothing could be
> said. (p. 97)

The moment, brought into being partly through language, is
beyond language and outside of time:

> It partook, she felt, carefully helping Mr Bankes to a specially
> tender piece, of eternity. . . . Of such moments, she thought, the
> thing is made that remains for ever after. This would remain.
>   'Yes', she assured William Bankes, 'there is plenty for
> everybody.' (p. 97)

With the verb 'partook' and the parenthetical 'carefully helping Mr
Bankes to a specially tender piece', Woolf ties the moment to the
dinner. Although we pause at the comma after 'piece', the eye
travels quickly enough that we also receive 'a specially tender piece
of eternity'. Woolf repeats the gambit at the end of the paragraph,
when she juxtaposes 'This would remain', with Mrs Ramsay's
assurance to Bankes, '"Yes, there is plenty for everybody"'; the
reader supplies the observation 'There is plenty [of the thing that
remains for ever] for everybody'. The slippage is deliberate,
linking the eternal and the temporal. The effect is double-edged:
the chunks of Boeuf en Daube partake of eternity even as they are

used to qualify Mrs Ramsay's claims for the permanence of the moment.

At the beginning of the dinner Mrs Ramsay had asked herself wearily, 'But what have I done with my life?' (p. 78); and Tansley certainly felt she had done nothing:

> They did nothing but talk, talk, talk, eat, eat, eat. It was the women's fault. Women made civilization impossible with all their 'charm', all their silliness. (p. 81)

In fact, working underneath whatever Tanley, Mr Ramsay, Carmichael and the others talk about, Mrs Ramsay has fused the group into a whole, forged for the moment a harmonious society. It is women, with all their talk – or rather what is conveyed beneath it – who make civilisation possible. It is this that Mrs Ramsay does with her life, and this that Carmichael's bow acknowledges.

We now regard Mrs Ramsay as a presence as well as a personality. The gathering seems suffused with her spirit, and the closing chant provides formal acknowledgement of her influence. The suggestions in the poetry of love and fertility ('The China rose is all abloom'), of the natural and the human cycles ('And all the lives we ever lived'), and of Christ ('To see the Kings ... With their palm leaves'), plus the associations with the Mass (it reminds Mrs Ramsay of 'Men and boys crying out the Latin words of a service in some Roman Catholic cathedral') broaden the significance of the occasion (pp. 102–3).[2] Carmichael then transfers this significance to Mrs Ramsay:

> Augustus Carmichael had risen and, holding his table napkin so that it looked like a long white robe he stood chanting ... and as she passed him he turned slightly towards her repeating the last words:
>
> Luriana, Lurilee
>
> and bowed to her as if he did her homage. (pp. 102–3)

The introduction of Carmichael adds to the consequence of the chant, and not simply because the description identifies him with a priest. He is distinguished by being the one character who seems immune to Mrs Ramsay's influence, the one whose thoughts are never reported to us, and the one whom we have not yet heard speak directly. Thus Carmichael's bow signifies the completion of harmony and affirms Mrs Ramsay's control.

Mrs Ramsay leaves the room in triumph, pausing to look back not only in space but in time, to a scene that is already the past:

> With her foot on the threshold she waited a moment longer in a scene which was vanishing even as she looked, and then, as she moved and took Minta's arm and left the room, it changed, it shaped itself differently; it had become, she knew, giving one last look at it over her shoulder, already the past.   (p. 103)

The sentence descends reluctantly, clause by clause, to the final word, 'past', acutely rendering the transience of things at the moment of fulfilment. When Mr Ramsay began his chant Mrs Ramsay 'knew it was poetry from the rhythm and the ring of exaltation and melancholy in his voice' (p. 102). Those are the two emotions that have informed the gathering, from the entrance of the lovers and the Boeuf en Daube: Mrs Ramsay feels the celebration of 'the love of man for woman' must be both 'profound' and mocking (p. 93); Lily sees this love as 'beautiful' and 'exciting' yet at the same time 'stupid' and 'barbaric' (p. 95). The Ramsays, she says, make you feel violently two opposite things at once. What they make you feel, we realise by the end of the dinner, is the contradictory nature, the exaltation and melancholy, of life itself.

Standing back for a moment, we can observe that Woolf's strategy has been to make Mrs Ramsay 'luminously transparent' not only through the reactions of the characters and by using obvious cues such as the imagery of the chant, but by narrating events in such a way that we see into them through Mrs Ramsay. By channelling these moments of insight through Mrs Ramsay, Woolf derives force from the concentration, and she also guarantees a receptiveness in her audience (that corresponds to Lily's readiness) to accept the reappearance of Mrs Ramsay as a revelation. Further, because the central figure has remained 'uncompromisingly solid' Woolf has prepared her audience for the 'ordinary' as well as the 'miraculous' quality of the vision.

The 'Time Passes' section exposes the fragility of Mrs Ramsay's triumph at the dinner-table. The phenomenal world asserts itself; chronological time becomes an inexorable force, combated only by the elemental Mrs McNab. The quest for reality dramatised in Mr Ramsay's intellectual attempt to reach the end of the alphabet (which founders, appropriately, as 'R', his own initial and emblem of the ego he cannot transcend) and Mrs Ramsay's mystical communion with the lighthouse (a traditional emblem of knowledge), is continued in this section by the figure of the 'searcher'. This searcher hopes to find

> some absolute good, some crystal of intensity . . . something alien to the processes of domestic life . . . which would render the possessor secure. (p. 123)

The searcher's quest is frustrated: there is no absolute, no escape from process, no security, and thus Lily takes up the quest at the beginning of Part III. 'What does it mean then, what can it all mean?' (p. 137), utilising the perceptual modes of both Ramsays and with at least a negative definition of what she is looking for. As she works on her painting she realises,

> The great revelation had never come. The great revelation perhaps never did come. Instead there were little daily miracles, illuminations, matches struck unexpectedly in the dark. . . . 'Mrs Ramsay! Mrs Ramsay!' she repeated. She owed this revelation to her. (pp.150–1)

Further, the revelation must incorporate both fact and vision:

> One wanted . . . to be on a level with ordinary experience, to feel simply that's a chair, that's a table, and yet at the same time, It's a miracle, it's an ecstasy. (p.186)

It is the whole complex being of Mrs Ramsay that she is trying to capture in the purple triangle on the canvas – a triangle that corresponds to the 'wedge of darkness', the hidden side of Mrs Ramsay which emerges in her encounter with the lighthouse, as well as to her more public talent for creating relationships, embodied in the triangular shape of the sock she is knitting.

As Lily sits before her painting she is intermittently beset by anguish for the loss of Mrs Ramsay, a feeling of inadequacy because she cannot give sympathy to Mr Ramsay, and frustration because she cannot achieve the desired harmony in her painting. Although they appear to be separate at first, the three problems are intimately related; and they are all resolved in the final vision. Her progress toward that vision is structured around the three cries of 'Mrs Ramsay! Mrs Ramsay!'

Lily's work proceeds, still hampered by her undischarged sympathy for Mr Ramsay and by her increasingly acute need for Mrs Ramsay. The elements of the scene she wishes to paint have become 'like curves and arabesques flourishing around a centre of complete emptiness' (p. 166); the missing element is Mrs Ramsay. She has become for Lily a force to shape the 'empty flourishes': 'Oh Mrs Ramsay! she called out silently, to that essence which sat by the boat, that abstract one made of her' (p. 165). She no longer thinks of her as a person who could guide one toward understanding; now Lily identifies her with meaning itself:

> Could it be, even for elderly people, that this was life? – startling, unexpected, unknown? For one moment she felt that if they both got up, here, now on the lawn and demanded an explanation . . . then, beauty would roll itself up; the space would fill; those empty flourishes would form into shape; if they shouted loud enough Mrs Ramsay would return. 'Mrs Ramsay!' she said aloud, 'Mrs Ramsay!' (p. 167)

Here the cry has a much greater emotional intensity than before, but it is the intensity of loss. The invocation (for we have learned to regard it as such) remains unanswered because, as Lily says a few moments later of her painting, 'One got nothing by soliciting urgently. . . . Let it come, she thought, if it will come' (pp. 178–9); these moments of being cannot be willed into existence. And in fact, Lily discovers that when her urgency to connect with Mrs Ramsay subsides, she feels a 'completeness' of the kind that ten years ago made her say 'she must be in love with the place' (p. 178). She considers how

> Love had a thousand shapes. There might be lovers whose gift it was to choose out the elements of things and place them together and so, giving them a wholeness not theirs in life, make of some scene, or meeting of people (all now gone and separate), one of those globed compacted things over which thought lingers, and love plays. (p. 178)

The phrase 'globed compacted thing' recalls the sonnet, and suggests that Lily is reaching the proper condition of ripeness – relaxed, undemanding, in harmony with the ethos of the place and no longer clutching at something specific – that will enable her to apprehend her subject.

She is thinking of Prue when a triangular shadow cast on the steps claims her attention. Although it is the shape that Mrs Ramsay made for the painting ten years ago, it does not arouse Lily's memory of her. Rather, she addresses herself to the quality of experience she wishes to capture and convey:

> One wanted, she thought, dipping her brush deliberately, to be on a level with ordinary experience, to feel simply that's a chair, that's a table, and yet at the same time, it's a miracle, it's an ecstasy. The problem might be solved after all.   (p. 186)

She will unite the fruits of both modes of perception (the example of a table is by now irrevocably associated with Mr Ramsay) in order to render the dual nature of reality. Thus prepared, she is at last granted her vision:

> Some wave of white went over the window pane. The air must have stirred some flounce in the room. Her heart leapt at her and seized her and tortured her.
> 'Mrs Ramsay! Mrs Ramsay!' she cried, feeling the old horror come back – to want and want and not to have. Could she inflict that still? And then, quietly, as if she refrained, that too became part of ordinary experience, was on a level with the chair, with the table. Mrs Ramsay – it was part of her perfect goodness to Lily – sat there quite simply, in the chair, flicked her needles to and fro, knitted her reddish-brown stocking, cast her shadow on the step. There she sat.   (p. 186)

Woolf ensures that the vision moves the reader too; Lily's wave of emotion comes to us through the rush of strong verbs in unpunctuated phrases ('her heart leapt at her and seized her and tortured her', 'feeling the old horror come back – to want and want and not to have'). Then a diminuendo of qualifying phrases brings us to a condition of calm and acceptance ('and then, quietly, as if she refrained, that too became part of ordinary experience, was on a level with the chair, with the table'). Finally, we receive the description of Mrs Ramsay: not with flowers in her hair as Lily has previously imagined her, but in her most characteristic pose, knitting. The ecstasy has been united with something completely ordinary.

The paragraph which gives Lily's vision best illustrates the

manner and the extent to which the reader is made to feel that
'nothing was simply one thing'. The cry 'Mrs Ramsay! Mrs Ramsay!' embodies the essence of the person named, and it contains the
horror and pain of the speaker, just as the corresponding cries did
in *The Voyage Out* and *Jacob's Room*. Yet the paragraph closes on a
statement of fulfilment and presence, 'There she sat', which echoes
the conclusion of *Mrs Dalloway*. However, 'For there she was', (*MD*,
172) is accompanied by Peter's 'terror', 'ecstasy' and 'extraordinary
excitement' – emotions that in the previous novels were generated
by the time-bound aspect of the relation. In *To the Lighthouse*, on the
other hand, the declaration, 'There she sat', has been drained of
excitement, to contain instead perfect serenity. The anguish of
personal loss succeeds to the fulfilment of complete union with the
being of the loved one, with that invisible and eternal core of
darkness. Thus the vision incorporates the veridical fact of ter-
mination in death with the reality of timeless being. Lily accepts the
perfect union offered her, without insisting (as Terence unreason-
ably does in *The Voyage Out*) that it endure.

However, the process of knowing is not yet complete, for Mrs
Ramsay's love engenders love, and Lily immediately moves to the
edge of the lawn to offer her sympathy to Mr Ramsay. When she
feels that he has received it, and Carmichael has consecrated the
moment with his embracing gesture, then finally she can complete
her painting – for a work of art is, in the broadest sense of the
word, an act of love. By having Lily repeat the words of Christ, 'It is
finished', and by comparing Carmichael to an 'old pagan God',
Woolf brings together Christian and pagan mythologies to extend
the significance of this 'ordinary miracle', making us feel that Mrs
Ramsay's love is eternally present (though seldom enough
grasped), that it transcends religious categories, that it is quite
simply, as Lily suggested earlier, necessary in order for 'the world
to go on at all' (p. 50). We feel with Lily that we have had our vision,
sensing, as Mrs Ramsay did with the sonnet, that we hold for a
moment the essence of life.

Painting and novel are completed together. The reader has long
since realised the one is proxy for the other. I have said that Lily
unites the perceptual modes of the two Ramsays, the intellectual –
rational – analytical with the intuitive – contemplative – mystical,
and Lily's description of her painting quoted earlier (like 'a
butterfly's wing' but clamped with 'bolts of iron') has been taken by
readers to be an account of what Woolf herself is trying to do in

literary terms. But Lily combines the qualities of the Ramsays in another sense as well. Mr Ramsay's search is wordy. Whether chanting 'The Charge of the Light Brigade', or looking forward to the lecture he will give in Cardiff ('his pleasure in it, in the phrases he made'),[3] or seeing all human knowledge as a great alphabet, his quest is relentlessly verbal. Mrs Ramsay's search, on the other hand, is wordless, the texts she weaves – her knitting, her dinners, her marriages – she accomplishes silently.

Lily unites language and silence, painting and writing, in her description of what the artist tries to do. As she struggles to capture Mrs Ramsay, 'Phrases came. Visions came. Beautiful pictures. Beautiful phrases', both of which seem to lead her toward 'the thing itself before it has been made anything' (p. 178). As Gayatri Spivak points out, Lily's desired discourse is 'a script, half design, half word, combining words and picturing: "Suddenly ... the whole wave and whisper of the garden became like curves and arabesques flourishing round a centre of complete emptiness"' (p. 275).[4]

Woolf's desired discourse, too, is one that flourishes round a centre of emptiness, that embodies some of the qualities of the plastic arts (at least metaphorically) as well as the literary. In her review of Dorothy Richardson's *Revolving Lights*, in which Woolf speaks of her 'psychological sentence of the feminine gender', she says,

> It is of a more elastic fibre than the old, capable of stretching to the extreme, of suspending the frailest particles, of enveloping the vaguest shapes.[5]

Some readers, like Sandra Gilbert and Michèle Barrett, have suggested that Woolf's notion of a 'female sentence' does not imply a different grammatical structure, but rather a different relation to language and a different subject matter. Others, such as Jane Marcus, argue that the 'absences, ellipses, ... the dot dot dot of unfinished sentences and uncompleted thoughts', as well as the rhythmic triple repetitions which characterise her prose, are aspects of this feminine style. And Luce Irigaray (not writing specifically of Woolf) imagines a female language 'which is constantly in the process of weaving itself, at the same time ceaselessly embracing words and yet casting them off to avoid becoming fixed, immobilized'.[6] All agree that silence lies at the heart of this language, that it constitutes an attempt to say what has not been said before, that cannot be said, but which needs words to lead to it. Several note that the *source* for this language lies in the words of the primitive woman, such as the beggar woman in *Jacob's Room* or *Mrs Dalloway*, or Mrs McNab in *To the Lighthouse*.

Yet that is not enough. Lily must give permanence to Mrs Ramsay's silent power to weave communion, and Woolf must give voice to these inchoate utterances. In *To the Lighthouse* Woolf forged a style capable of embracing the voices of the individual characters, of enveloping eternity and Bouef en Daube, of suspending time for a moment as the dinner part fades, of rendering the jolt and serenity of Lily's vision. She fashioned a sentence that, while not a new grammatical unit, and not a cry, nevertheless breaks the expected order (as she says in *A Room of One's Own*), a sentence which taps the resources of silence in language and which has the elasticity and the capacity for suspending and enveloping, rather than ordering and fixing, that she regarded as distinctively 'feminine'.[7]

The Waves: 'A fin in a waste of waters'

To the reader coming at *The Waves* after *To the Lighthouse* the change is drastic. It is another novel with a quest, but there is no sea voyage to structure the quest, and no plot and no characters in the conventional sense.[1] We overhear six voices, but this is certainly not stream of consciousness or even indirect interior monologue. The vocabulary and style do not change from character to character, nor does the language alter with the age of the characters (as it does so strikingly in Joyce's *Portrait of the Artist*, which begins as *The Waves* does with the dawning of consciousness in character). We are not in the consciousness of the characters, perceiving with them; we receive through some narrating consciousness the reported record of the character talking/thinking his or her experience.[2] The mode is never truly dramatic: the characters do not talk to each other. When in the ninth section we suddenly encounter the avuncular tone of Bernard's summation, adopted for the acquaintance across the table, we realise how stylized the mode has been.

The most striking departure from the conventional mode of the novel is in the verb tenses. The narrating voice uses the pure present rather than the progressive; thus we are presented with 'I see a ring' rather than 'I am watching a ring'. It is the tense usually reserved for external acts with no fixed time, or for repeated actions, or for internal events exempt from time, such as, 'I believe'. This makes the events seem momentary, giving them an urgency they would not otherwise possess, and whether this mode is specifically 'feminine', as Pamela Transue argues, in that it reinforces the potential for 'moments of being' which male characters do not have, it does as she says intensify the present moment.[3] The relentless intensity of the book (which makes it something that should be read in short concentrated bursts, like poetry, rather than in the relaxed, collusive mode one can adopt even with novels like *To the Lighthouse*) derives from the fact that every utterance is in effect a 'moment of being'. '"Now Biddy scrapes the fish-scales with a jagged knife on to a wooden board"' (p. 7), Neville tells us, not as part of an account of that evening's dinner, but as something as absolute, gnomic, almost as portentous as his vision of 'death among the apple tree' (p. 17). Further, the use of the pure present adds to the incantatory feel of the speeches, conveying the sense of something chanted rather than spoken, raising the whole discourse to the level of ritual, the plane which the action of *To the Lighthouse* achieves momentarily with the completion of the dinner and the completion of the painting.

In her *Diary* Woolf referred to the work as a 'play-poem' (III, 203), and the book does combine the forward movement expected of drama with the simultaneity associated with lyric poetry. The progression of chronological time, which is created externally by the interludes and within the episodes by the declared ageing of the characters, asserts the horizontal moment. Opposing this motion is the absence of causality in the story, the frequent echoes which arrest the reader, and a durational time that is maintained by the use of the present tense.

These conflicting 'play-poem' qualities of sequence and simultaneity characterise the form of the discourse and the concept of character as well. The uniform narrative voice denies one the sense of sharp definition (and thus also of chronological progression) when moving from speaker to speaker. Woolf enhances this verbal blurring of the characters' edges by never beginning with, for example, 'Bernard said, "..."'; we must always read into a speech before learning who the speaker is. And though we quickly become aware that each character has favourite images for experience – Bernard's bubbles, Rhoda's square upon an oblong – we discover that phrases of one speaker will appear in the soliloquy of another. Thus the text supports the speculations put forward by Bernard (a more complex version of those by Clarissa Dalloway) on the fluidity of identity. In addition to reinforcing the notion of a fundamental unity among human beings, the suggestion of a shared pool of images (along with the uniform tone) gives the impression that these speeches are contained within a single embracing consciousness. Yet the terse markers, 'Louis said', 'Rhoda said', 'Jinny said', administer a jolt with each switch in speaker. Thus in spite of the details which persuade the reader that these characters are aspects

of one character, *The Waves*, unlike the previous novels, deliberately keeps the reader aware of the lines of demarcation between
speakers.

Also, the narrator never varies the introductory epithets for the
speeches, always using 'said' rather than 'thought', 'cried',
'lamented' or other similarly specific verbs which would blur the
distinction between the fiction and the narration as in a traditional
novel. Further, the self-consciousness of the narrator appears in a
more overt use of *leitmotifs* than Woolf's novels have demonstrated
before, as well as in a deliberate use of incantatory phrases, such as
'The beast stamps', used by both Louis and the narrator. So
deliberate is this device that the narrating consciousness treats it
ironically. One of the more haunting phrases in the book is Louis's
prophetic 'Death is woven in with the violets. . . . Death and again
death' (p. 95). Yet the narrator here undercuts the intensity of the
phrase with the same character's worried statement, 'I sign my
name, I, I, and again I' (pp. 115, 112); and she mocks it outright
with Bernard's grumbling over the menu of a Cumberland inn:
'nothing but mutton and mutton and again mutton' (p. 173).

In her other books Woolf sought to submerge her 'scaffolding';
here she asserts it. And although convenience must have prompted
her to do otherwise, she maintains the novel's convention for
presenting direct speech. Woolf could have emulated Hardy's
play-poem, *The Dynasts*, and set off the soliloquies in the manner of
dramatic literature; or she could have done as Joyce did and
eliminated quotation marks while keeping the conventional layout
of the novel. But Joyce wished to eliminate their distraction and
here the intrusion serves Woolf's purpose, for appearing as they
do at the beginning of each paragraph, whether it contains
dialogue, conscious thought or a rendering of deeper levels of
consciousness, the marks constantly remind us that what we are
receiving is a transcription. Further, the vestiges of the novel form
keep the reader in mind of what the book is not. Neither play, nor
poem, nor novel, though with qualities of each, the work, for all its
crystalline aspect, is in the process of searching for a form.

Beneath the rigid scaffolding, what gives the book life is the
rhythm of the waves. In June of 1929 when *The Waves* was still 'The
Moths' and Woolf had not yet begun to write but was letting the
book grow in her mind, she wondered, 'Could one not get the
waves to be heard all through?' Yet in the next sentence she goes
on, 'Or the farmyard noises? Some odd irrelevant noises' (*D* III,

236). In the event, the waves were hardly as peripheral as these musings suggest, and certainly Woolf too knew that at the time. But the book would go through many changes before it reached its final form, and the waves, referred to in the same diary entry as 'phantom waves', gained force not as phenomena but as governing metaphor. For in fact we don't 'hear' the waves so much as intuit their shaping presence throughout the book.

The waves are there in the interludes, of course, from the pleasantly anthropomorphic opening, where 'each bar rose, heaped itself, broke and swept a thin veil of white water across the sand.... sighing like a sleeper whose breath comes and goes unconsciously' to the final chilling line, 'The waves broke on the shore.' But the book is also an extended discussion of character, and the six 'characters' are both separate and one, like the waves, individual and distinct yet merging in the sea. Further, the metaphor of the waves controls the shape of the discourse. The six voices, often compared to a chorus, are separate but not completely individualised: they are like waves that merge in the sea of Bernard's summation, which incorporates even the language of the interludes.

This much is obvious. But the waves also work beneath the surface of the text, giving it its rhythm. The rhythm is, in the broad sense, that of life. The book moves from dawn to dusk, from youth to maturity, with the waves serving as a kind of cosmic metronome, marking the inexorable and indifferent passage of time. However, if this were the only rhythm the book would quickly become tedious. Milan Kundera, writing on rhythm, says,

> I hate to hear the beat of my heart; it is a relentless reminder that the minutes of my life are numbered. So I have always seen something macabre in the bar lines that measure out a musical score. But the greatest masters of rhythm know how to silence that monotonous and predictable regularity, and transform their music into a little enclave of 'time outside time'.

Woolf wants that reminder of death (though she did not regard it as 'macabre'; her characters are defined or define themselves in terms of death), yet her book succeeds in creating that enclave outside of time, an enclave which all the characters *in* the book try vainly to construct. Kundera goes on,

In late Beethoven, the rhythm is so complicated, especially in the slow movements, that we can barely make out the bar lines.[4]

Woolf herself listened to the late Beethoven quartets while she was composing *The Waves* (*D* iii, 139, 339), and while it is impossible to document a direct correspondence, there is a complexity to the rhythm of this book not found in her other novels.[5]

Part of the subtlety derives from her handling of the waves and the other physical phenomena of the interludes. As Avrom Fleishman points out, there is a common structure to these interludes – paragraph one focuses on the sea's appearance and the waves, paragraph two on the garden and the response of the birds, paragraph three on the light through the house – but the pattern holds exactly only for the first two interludes before it is varied.[6] Thus Woolf blurs what Kundera would call the 'bar lines' (a metaphor latent in Woolf's visual description of the waves). Further, the particulars quickly build up a complex of associations that takes us far beyond the simple metaphors of the sea of life, or life as a day. By the third interlude the narrator has moved into Homeric simile:

> As [the waves] splashed and drew back they left a black rim of twigs and cork on the shore and straws and sticks of wood, as if some light shallop had foundered and burst its sides and the sailor had swum to land and bounded up the cliff and left his frail cargo to be washed ashore. (p. 49)

And there is something more going on in the interludes. This simile creates a scene, but like all similes it is a comparison in which the logic is apparent, the process of association, however ingenious, easily followed – the waves strew scraps of wood and cork on the beach in a way that makes one think of a shipwreck (to much diminish Woolf's figure). But look at the last paragraph of the same interlude:

> The waves drummed on the shore, like turbaned warriors, like turbaned men with poisoned assegais who, whirling their arms on high, advance upon the feeding flocks, the white sheep. (p. 51)

Here the connections are more oblique. The reader does not

visualise the waves in the shape of warriors, nor imagine the white froth on the waves as the turbans, or, after breaking, as the sheep. This is, as it were, Homeric metaphor, for the scene created is more than an elaborate comparison; it is rendering something inaccessible to denotative prose. Then in Interlude 4 the image returns in a conventional simile:

> Their spray rose like the tossing of lances and assegais over the riders' heads.   (p. 73)

Thus Woolf blurs the bar lines with the action of the discourse itself, which embodies another wave-like rhythm, a movement in and out of metaphor. The book is also musical in being sequential but not referential (at least not referential in the sense one usually associates with the novel), and in possessing that capacity for swift unprepared change which characterises music and lyric poetry. The waves, then, even while functioning as a visual image infuse their rhythm into all aspects of the text, from concepts of character, to modes of discourse, to levels of figurative language. It is there as well, of course, in the emotional rise and fall of the characters.

These emotions are, to a remarkable degree, associated with language, as the characters themselves struggle to create form with words. *The Waves* is, as Fleishman points out, a sustained meditation on the nature of the self, and Bernard actively theorises about it.[7] But the struggle to define the self is inseparable from the struggle with language. Most of the commentary on language comes from Bernard, whose passion for phrases is his defining characteristic, but in fact all the characters concern themselves with words.

Even in the first episode, the characters all have definite attitudes toward their Latin verbs, from Bernard who regards them as living things – 'They flick their tails; they move through the air in flocks' – to Neville who sees them as embodiments of order – 'There is an order in this world, there are distinctions, there are differences in this world' (p. 14).

As they grow older three of the characters, Neville, Louis and Bernard, strive to become artists. At school Neville develops his passion for Catullus, and he also comes to recognise that his enthusiasm is too exclusively intellectual. When he reads to Percival he sees that he understands more than Louis. Not the words, but what are the words? Do I not know already how to rhyme, how to imitate Pope, Dryden, even Shakespeare? . . . I shall be a clinger to the outsides of words all my life. (p. 32)

Thus he becomes 'the most slavish of students', destined sedulously to 'follow the curve of the sentence wherever it might lead, into deserts, under drifts of sand', into the often arid tracts of scholarship.

Louis reiterates the need for the poet to have more than a facility with words. At school he has a 'sudden perception' of 'some other order, and better, which makes a reason everlastingly':

This I see for a second, and shall try to-night to fix in words, to forge in a ring of steel, though Percival destroys it as he blunders off. . . . Yet it is Percival I need; for it is Percival who inspires poetry. (p. 27)

Poetry must include that raw vitality of life (which Percival embodies and represents), the quality which is least submissive to the constraints of language. In spite of the difficulty, the ring of steel must be forged, for if the poet does not realise the vision in language the entire cultural tradition suffers:

I force myself to state, if only in one line of unwritten poetry, this moment . . . . But if I now shut my eyes, if I fail to realise the meeting-place of past and present . . . human history is defrauded of a moment's vision. Its eye, that would see through me, shuts . . . . (p. 45)

However, Louis's poem goes unwritten. His insecurity drives him to seek success in commerce and so instead of writing poetry he signs his name, 'I, and again I', on business letters.

The other characters cast doubt upon the ability of language to do what they ask of it. Rhoda complains that images obscure rather than reveal: '"Like" and "like" and "like" – but what is the thing that lies beneath the semblance of the thing?' (p. 110). Susan, who understands only 'cries of love, hate, rage and pain,' anticipates Bernard's wish to do away with words:

This talking is undressing an old woman whose dress had

seemed to be part of her, but now, as we talk, she turns pinkish underneath, and has wrinkled thighs and sagging breasts. When you are silent you are again beautiful. (p. 88)

Jinny alone expresses no dissatisfaction with words, but only because she never lingers with them: 'I cannot follow any word through its changes' (p. 28). Although she, like Bernard, makes up stories about people she quickly becomes impatient. For Jinny all words are variations of the single call, 'Come': 'Crowding, like a fluttering bird, one sentence crosses the empty space between us. It settles on his lips. . . . I am admitted to the warmth and privacy of another soul' (p. 70).

Bernard, of course, is the compulsive and profligate phrase-maker, and the development of his character is measured in terms of his changing attitude toward language. From childhood he has been a spinner of tales, and that the tales inevitably go unfinished does not deter him. Gradually he learns that he lacks the detachment of the artist, and that phrases 'require some final refrigeration which I cannot give them, dabbling always in warm soluble words' (p. 46). Later he questions the presence of an order in existence that corresponds to the events of his narratives:

But what are stories? Toys I twist, bubbles I blow, one ring passing through another. And sometimes I begin to doubt if there are stories. . . . There are facts, as, for example: 'The handsome young man . . . made a sign to the waiter, who came instantly and returned a moment later with the bill discreetly folded upon a plate.' That is the truth; that is the fact, but beyond it all is darkness and conjecture. (p. 97)

By the end of the book, it will be this sense of 'darkness and conjecture', rather than any story, that he seeks to realise in language.

With the death of Percival, Bernard for the first time feels that 'I need silence . . . . Now then is my chance to find out what is of great importance, and I must be careful, and tell no lies' (p. 103). Bernard does continue to make phrases, but he questions them more strongly. In middle age he reflects, 'I have filled innumerable notebooks with phrases to be used when I have found the true story . . . . But I have never yet found that story. And I begin to ask, Are there stories?' The more emphatic tone ('Are there stories?')

and the scepticism as he goes on to ask 'But why impose my
arbitrary design? ... Why select this out of all that?' (pp. 126–7)
indicates a deepening conviction that any ordering is false. At the
end of the book, in a passage that recalls Prospero and anticipates
Beckett, he lets his phrase-book drop to the floor and declares:

> I need a little language such as lovers use, words of one syllable
> such as children speak.... I need a howl; a cry. When the storm
> crosses the marsh and sweeps over me where I lie in the ditch
> unregarded I need no words. Nothing neat. Nothing that comes
> down with all its feet on the floor. None of those resonances and
> lovely echoes that break and chime from nerve to nerve in our
> breasts, making wild music, false phrases. I have done with
> phrases. (p. 199)

However, to back-track for a moment, a few moments after
asking 'Why select ... one detail?' Bernard insists upon the power
of a single image to body forth meaning. It is the image that lies at
the heart of *The Waves*, touchstone both for Bernard and for
Virginia Woolf:

> Leaning over this parapet [he is on holiday in Rome] I see far out
> a waste of water. A fin turns. This bare visual impression is
> unattached to any line of reason, it springs up as one might see
> the fin of a porpoise on the horizon. Visual impressions often
> communicate thus briefly statements that we shall in time to
> come uncover and coax into words. I note under F., therefore,
> 'Fin in a waste of waters'.

He continues,

> Now I shall go and lunch somewhere.... I shall observe with
> more than my usual detachment, and when a pretty woman
> enters ... I shall say to myself, 'Look where she comes against a
> waste of waters.' A meaningless observation, but to me, solemn,
> slate-coloured, with a fatal sound of ruining worlds and waters
> falling to destruction. (pp. 127–8)

The significant characteristic of this impression is that it has come
unbidden and 'unattached to any line of reason'. It exists in the
mind entire, neither evasive nor 'soluble' in the manner of so many

of his phrases, and inexhaustibly resonant while at the same time inaccessible to logical analysis. When he comments upon the 'waste of waters' he does so in figurative language: 'solemn, slate-coloured, with a fatal sound of ruining worlds and waters falling to destruction' is further evocative of desolation, yet it remains, logically, a 'meaningless observation'. In saying that 'in time to come' one may 'coax' these impressions into words, Bernard does not mean that the image can be expressed with any greater lucidity or precision – it is fused with the experience and therefore irreducible – but rather that he may be able, in the context of a work of art, to invest it with the same immediacy and significance that it holds for him at this moment, thereby making it accessible to others. Bernard never succeeds, but *The Waves* was Woolf's sustained meditation upon that image, her attempt to coax the implications of it into words.

In her *Diary* for 30 September 1926 Woolf records the vision. The entry is worth quoting at length because it contains to a remarkable degree the central impulses of the book published five years later.

> I wished to add some remarks to this, on the mystical side of this solitude; how it is not oneself but something in the universe that one's left with. It is this that is frightening and exciting in the midst of my profound gloom, depression, boredom, whatever it is. One sees a fin passing far out. What image can I reach to convey what I mean? Really there is none I think.

The fin represents the 'mystical side' of solitude, the solitude Bernard praises extravagantly near the end of his summation. It is something both frightening and yet exciting. And Woolf cannot find an image to convey what she means. Significantly, the image must be rendered by an image: the fin cannot be reduced to, for instance, a flash of 'being' in the sea of 'non-being' that is daily life. She goes on,

> Life is, soberly & accurately, the oddest affair; has in it the essence of reality. I used to feel this as a child – couldn't step across a puddle once I remember, for thinking, how strange – what am I? &c. But by writing I don't reach anything. All I mean to make is a note of a curious state of mind. I hazard the guess that it may be the impulse behind another book. At present my

mind is totally blank & virgin of books. [Here she has a marginal note, 'Perhaps the Waves or moths (Oct. 1929)] I want to watch and see how the idea at first occurs. I want to trace my own process.   (*D* III, 113)

Here she relates the vision of the fin to the nature of 'reality' and to her sense of the self, in a memory that recalls Neville's vision of death among the apple tree. Thus, as in the finished book, notions of reality in general, the self in particular, and language as the means of coming at them, are united in the constellation of images related to the fin.

On 7 February 1931 when she finished the second draft she recorded, with 'triumph & relief',

> Whether good or bad, its done; & as I certainly felt at the end, not merely finished, but rounded off, completed, the thing stated – how hastily, how fragmentarily I know; but I mean that I have netted that fin in the waste of waters . . .   (*D* IV, 10)[8]

She feels that she has 'stated' the thing, coaxed the meaning of the experience behind that image into words at last. However, when she wrote this she had actually eliminated the vision of the fin from *The Waves*. She retained it only as an incidental image Bernard coins to describe his conversation with Neville. Clearly she felt that she could communicate the power of the original vision without the image itself. Yet between this draft and the published text she would insert the passage quoted above in which Bernard sees the fin turning in the waste of waters. Tracing the vision from the *Diary* through the drafts to the published text helps illuminate how the image finally works.

In the first draft it is Rhoda who has the vision of the fin. After Percival's death she says,

> This is my reality. . . .
>   passing, like a dark fin . . .
>   Then I am drawn, very unwillingly, always
>   through a waste of loneliness, of despair, when everything
>   has failed, when I have no existence & it is my fate
>   to have no existence, ~~no stability~~, no natural
>   happiness: ~~then I~~ I achieve this solace, for a
>   moment some <vision> ~~union~~ . . .

which has its solace; ~~with something that am aware of~~
~~some un-existence not ours~~ . . .
. . . & in order to hoard
this painful sense, I would ~~sacrifice all my friend~~s; I
would have no interruption.   (*HDW* I, 258; I have omitted
some deletions)

The vision is powerful; like the vision Woolf records in her *Diary* it
is linked with a loss of self ('when I have no existence') and a union
with some greater reality ('some existence not ours'), and though it
is something she is drawn into 'unwillingly' because it takes her
'through a waste of loneliness, of despair', it is yet something that
she would 'sacrifice' all her friends to, or at least not have
interrupted. For it gives her, she says a few lines later, 'a sense of
nothingness' that she values for her ceremony of dropping violets
into the sea in honour of Percival. In Draft I Bernard uses the
image of the fin only for his talk with Neville:

we sank into one of those stupors that are more fertile than talk,
when ~~some~~ fin rises, here & there . . . & it sinks back, leaving a
little ripple of curiosity.   (*HDW* I, 378)

In Draft II Rhoda's vision disappears altogether, replaced by the
square upon the oblong (*HDW* II, 578; *W*, 110). Bernard again uses
the image for his conversation with Neville, but again it is associated only with 'stupor', 'satisfaction' and contentment (*HDW* II,
706; *W*, 184), reminding us of Jacob's conversation with Simeon at
Cambridge. Indeed the experience seems less profound than that
recorded in *Jacob's Room*; the value of the conversation is only felt
when we catch the echo of Bernard's vision. The paragraph that
will later become a full paragraph describing the vision is in Draft
II just a marginal variant: 'these visions of fins' is considered along
with 'these moments of escape', 'these elevated prospects', 'these
glimpses' (*HDW* II, 615; *W*, 128). And in the section in which
Bernard describes the desolate vision of a world seen without a self
there is no reference at all to the fin, which in the final text defines
his state:

I cried then with a sudden conviction of complete desertion.
Now there is nothing. No fin breaks the waste of this immeasur-
able sea. Life has destroyed me. No echo comes when I speak, no
varied words.   (p. 192)

Once again we note the complex of reality, being and language. But in Draft II, though Woolf includes almost all the other elements of the experience she ignores the fin. Why does she add it between the second draft and the published text?

It is as if Woolf recognised, after announcing in her *Diary* at the end of Draft II that she had 'netted her fin in the waste of water', that in spite of her efforts to paraphrase it or do without it, the image itself could not be ignored. And so leaving it in the comparatively shallow context of the conversation between Bernard and Neville, she restored the passage which makes the image expressive of a truth which is compelling and whose value is self-evident, but which cannot be explained.

But why give it now to Bernard rather than to Rhoda? And why move it from its original charged context, the death of Percival? The first question is easily answered, for even in Rhoda's version the experience is associated with death but also with a rebirth; one returns to the world restored, and her suicide would alter the meaning of the vision. Further, Bernard is the phrase-maker, and the function of the phrase itself is important.

Why make it part of Bernard's experience in Rome, where he is 'shedding one of [his] life-skins' (p. 127), the vision no longer linked to the death of Percival? It is, I would suggest, crucial that the fin *not* be related to Percival. He is the centre of the novel, but to leave the fin with him, as it was in Draft I, would be to reduce it to a specific occasion. Not only is the fin no longer associated with the death of Percival, it is not connected specifically to the obliteration of the self, as it was for Rhoda. Indeed, its connection with Bernard's 'eclipse' of personality is now the opposite of what it was in the draft: it defines something impersonal that he measures his self against. *The Waves* is often described as the most impersonal of Woolf's books; that quality was developed through the drafts and it guided her revisions between the draft and the published text. We are distanced because we are not meant to identify with a character but with an experience, an emotion. If we became interested in the psychological repercussions of the vision we would be diverted from the experience of being itself. Even though in *To the Lighthouse* the mystical experience is dramatised rather than described, it remains in part an element in the characterising of Mrs Ramsay. Giving it to Bernard, connecting it to the nature of self-hood and being, and making it something that comes unsolicited and unrelated to any personal crisis, Woolf evokes the impersonal aspect of the vision that generated the book itself.

Bernard himself can do comparatively little with the image; he can *define* what he needs, but he remains too analytical to craft that little language he calls for. This strategy is deliberate on Woolf's part. It does not constitute a denial of art (which, of course, we could counter with the familiar argument that this denial is subverted by the existence of the text itself so that Woolf affirms art whether she wants to or not), but as a means of maintaining the impersonality. It has been argued that *The Waves* does deny the power of art, and it is true that of the six characters three are literary artists (Louis and Neville write poetry) and all fail. Further, although after Percival's death Bernard finds a certain solace in the National Gallery looking at Titian (p. 105), and Rhoda at the opera where the players 'take the square and place it upon the oblong' (p. 110), ultimately the aesthetic ordering is insufficient in the face of death. Art is powerless against the obliteration of the individual; the waves will always break on the shore. But art can put one in contact with that greater reality behind things, a reality in which the individual ego is lost and life and death merge. Art fails the characters in the book because they are asking it to do the wrong thing.

Woolf does what Bernard cannot, she elaborates the image so that for us too it becomes a vehicle for entering into reality. The experience is a moment of being, the image of the fin is the means of yielding its full potentiality to the one who experiences it (Neville tries to do this with his more prosaic phrase 'death among the apple trees'), the book is the means of communicating it to others. And what is communicated is, of course, nothing conclusive; it is the profound and paradoxical experience that prompts meditation. Graham argues that the book is a sustained visionary search, that there are moments of revelation as there are for Clarissa Dalloway or Mrs Ramsay, that the characters throughout sift experience for the fragments of reality.[9] Woolf's art succeeds because it involves us in that search, haunts us with that image. Woolf finally nets the fin by communicating its inexhaustible and irreducible nature, by freeing it from personality, allowing its connection with universal reality to emerge.

In the final section Bernard reviews the events of his life, but from the outset his account is also a consideration of whether one can communicate the experience of living, both how to record daily life and how to net the fin of the reality underlying it. He begins positively enough, 'Now to sum up. . . . Now to explain to you the meaning of my life'; but almost immediately the qualifications and disclaimers begin: 'The illusion is upon me that something adheres . . . . This, for the moment, seems to be my life. If it were possible I would hand it you entire' (pp. 160–1). Bernard thus sets the patterns for his summation, in which he restlessly qualifies any conclusion. His oscillations stem not from confusion but from his refusal to simplify. He states the problem flatly for his silent interlocutor: 'in order to make you understand, to give you my life, I must tell you a story – and there are so many . . . and none of them are true' (p. 161). No matter how formless the experience he wishes to communicate is, he must impose some sort of form.

Bernard confronts the paradox of life by making paradox a basic mode of procedure in his summation. He expresses his longing for 'broken words, inarticulate words' with supreme articulateness, and he uses brilliant phrases to deny the meretriciousness of words: 'I need no words. . . . None of those resonances and lovely echoes that break and chime from nerve to nerve in our breasts, making wild music, false phrases' (p. 199). Further, while denying sequences – 'All these things happen in one second and last forever' (p. 162) – he opens his *recit* proper in the manner of a chronicle, 'In the beginning' and he continues using strong temporal hypotaxis: 'Then, there was a garden . . . . I then first became aware . . . . But let me dip again . . . . Neville next . . .' (pp. 161–5). Yet he soon begins to use sequence itself to subvert the linear quality of his narrative, repeating for instance his phrase for the sequential life, 'Tuesday follows Monday' (pp. 174, 177, 181, 183, 191) until it creates a sense of simultaneity among moments. The repetitions also start to empty the phrase of logical meaning, so that it becomes primarily a rhythmic device which charts Bernard's emotional rise and fall.

Nevertheless, this self-consciousness is itself explicitly challenged by the form of Bernard's summation. Here a genuine dramatic monologue supplants the juxtaposed soliloquies of the disembodied chorus that has presented the text thus far. We know for example that Bernard met his acquaintance at the coat-check closet, that as they sit Bernard has his back to the door and is facing a mirror, that they had fowl with wine for dinner and pears with brandy for dessert. For the first time we see Bernard, although sketchily, from the outside: he is 'rather heavy, elderly . . . grey at the temples', and he cradles his old brandy in his left hand (pp. 161, 197). In his narrative he uses the conventional past tense. Thus even though he repeatedly states that such stories are fraudulent, it is as if we are now to be convinced by the illusion, rather than reminded of the artifice as we have been previously.

However, the ninth section demands a reassessment of the whole book, not merely an adjustment for its more conventional form. Each mode of presentation exposes the inherent distortions of the other. Bernard acknowledges the uses of the biographic style, and his summation, which is more sequential than what has gone before, strikes us as a valid way of dealing with the events of his life. Yet what he appears to be working towards, with his various endeavours to subvert the sequence of narrative, is something like the soliloquies we have just read, for they confess their patterning with every word, and in avowing the arbitrary selection of the artist they avoid the implication of a natural order in existence. The soliloquies would seem then to provide an answer to Bernard's complaints about the plausible order created by phrases. However, Bernard does not, like Marcel at the end of Proust's *Remembrance of Things Past*, decide to write the novel we have just read. There is no discovery of a form or a language; in *To the Lighthouse* Woolf had taken seamless narration about as far as it could go. Now she challenges it, not by self-conscious questioning, as in *Jacob's Room*, but by setting up a collision of modes that is itself metaphoric.

The ending resembles those of the other novels, in which the forces of the work of art converge upon a single moment of vision. Bernard's voice subsumes the other voices, drawing together the themes and motifs, and continuing the wave motion that has been present in the prose rhythms and in the emotional rise and fall of the speakers. His emotional fluctuations become greater and greater until exaltation and despair lose their separate meanings and merge in the final cry, 'O Death!', which realises Bernard's perception of the complete fulfilment and of the complete obliteration that must occur in a full engagement with being.

However, this book departs from the other novels in the austerity of the ending and of the work as a whole. In *The Waves* the author focuses on the relation between mind and being rather than upon human relationships. And Bernard's cry completes the drift toward pure being that has been evident in the successive endings of the earlier novels. 'Rachel! Rachel!' realised the essence of a character and, by implication, being; 'Mrs Ramsay! Mrs Ramsay!' captured the sense of the individual and of abstract being in equal

measure; in 'O Death!' Woolf directs our attention beyond individuals to a more impersonal relation.

The theme of human communion is still prominent in *The Waves*,
but the emphasis invariably falls upon its transience. At the
farewell dinner the characters attempt 'to make one thing, not
enduring – for what endures? – but seen by many eyes simultaneously' (p. 85); and after the reunion dinner Bernard says, 'let
us behold what we have made. Let it blaze out against the yew trees.
One life. There. It is over. Gone out' (p. 155). In spite of his claim
that these things happen in one second and last for ever, in *The
Waves* communion is always fragmentary and evanescent. Concom-
itantly the attraction of that 'no-man's land' where one becomes
'deep, tideless, immune' and 'unconfined' becomes more potent.
Bernard's cry bodies forth the conjunction of meaning and
meaninglessness: thus to speak of it as affirming or surrendering is
to limit it. It is a cry of recognition that captures the limits of
knowing.

Through Bernard, Woolf enacts the progressive disillusionment
with language that we have traced in her novels. His early
confidence in phrases recalls the eager optimism of Terence in *The
Voyage Out* who was to write the novel 'about Silence, the things
people don't say'. During the period in which he discovers that
words seem less amenable than he expected, Bernard resembles
the narrator of *Jacob's Room* who complained that words get the
wrong accent on them. For both the feeling still remained that if
one could handle words correctly they would capture reality. By
middle age his sentiments correspond to those expressed in *To the
Lighthouse*: serious questioning of language combined with a
guarded confidence that it is possible to embody and communicate
one's vision.

The experience of losing his contemplative self radically alters
Bernard's perspective. Having felt himself to be almost nonexistent
without an audience he now finds a meaningful relation only with
being. Language is no longer to be used to create and communicate
order but to bring one face to face with that region beyond
language where 'all is darkness and conjecture' (p. 103). This is
what *The Waves* attempts to do. In our engagement with the work
of art we join the author not in human communion but only as
fellow confronters of being – hence the convention of the soliloquies. The members of the chorus do not face each other, or the
audience, but being; and we overhear. Bernard's summation

exemplifies the familiar climactic movement toward a charged primitive cry that impels the reader beyond language, but in the soliloquies Woolf does something new. In them every statement moves past us into silence, and language becomes almost pure pattern. T. S. Eliot accurately describes the condition in 'Burnt Norton':

> Words, after speech, reach
> Into the silence. Only by the form, the pattern,
> Can words or music reach
> The stillness, as a Chinese jar still
> Moves perpetually in its stillness.[10]

In *The Waves* Woolf goes to her furthest extreme in exploring the limits of language. She brings herself and the reader into a stark encounter with being, and she strains the form of her art until finally, in its extreme stylisation, it takes on some of the mysterious muteness of a physical artefact, a silence such as Eliot's Chinese jar possesses – or that of a fin moving soundlessly in a waste of waters.

Between the Acts: The 'Orts, Scraps and Fragments' of Postmodernism

Between the Acts has probably occasioned a more disparate critical response than any other of Woolf's major novels. From the outset readers have disagreed over whether the mood of the book is bleak and despairing (with the odd light touch) or affirmative and comic (with dark strains running through it).[1] The book is difficult to get a handle on: it is no longer a voyage, whether 'out' or 'to the lighthouse'; it no longer focuses on a particular character, her parties or his room; it no longer invokes the linear flow of waves or years. The title, as L. J. Swingle points out, evolved in the drafts from 'Pointz Hall', which suggests a walled-in structure apart from the temporal process, to 'The Pageant', which forces acknowledgement of that process even as it attempts to transform mere change into coherent acts, to the final title, 'Between the Acts', which places the emphasis on the abyss between any two elements of a given enclosure. Taken most literally, the title privileges the actions that takes place in the intervals between the acts of the country pageant.[2]

But the title evokes wider associations. The action takes place on a June day in 1939, at a moment when all were conscious of being poised between two world wars. The interlude is also that between the acts of love of Giles and Isa, whose conflict is emblematic of the larger conflict between nations. In terms of world history, Lucy's reflections on prehistoric times reduce human civilisation to an interlude between the acts of nonhuman dominance of the earth. On the individual level, life is, of course, the pageant between birth and death, and we live between the acts, in a shifting ground between private and public worlds.[3] And within the book itself, there are the interludes between speech acts, silences of void and of plenum, silences both generative and arid.

Silence lies at the heart of this book, more prominent and more potent than in other novels. The passage that haunts our reading of the book is the description of the dining-room. The room is at the heart of the country house, and, by extension, at the heart of society. In *To the Lighthouse* the dining-room had a similar significance, but there the candles and the bowl of fruit provided the physical framework for a communion that held against the dissolution and darkness outside. Here the physical objects, two portraits and a vase, lead one toward that chaos outside. One portrait is of an ancestor, the other, bought by Oliver because he liked it, is 'a picture':

> He was a talk producer, that ancestor. But the lady was a picture. In her yellow robe, leaning, with a pillar to support her, a silver arrow in her hand, and a feather in her hair, she led the eye up, down, from the curve to the straight, through glades of greenery and shades of silver, dun and rose into silence. The room was empty.
>
> Empty, empty, empty; silent, silent, silent. The room was a shell, singing of what was before time was; a vase stood in the heart of the house, alabaster, smooth, cold, holding the still, distilled essence of emptiness, silence.   (p. 31)

Mrs Ramsay's cornucopia has been replaced by a vase of chilling purity, enclosing a void.

Similarly, Isa's moment of being is characterised by an inhuman silence. In capping quotations with Mrs Manresa, Isa completes 'To be or not to be' with 'the first words that came into her head': Keats's address to the Nightingale: '"Fade far away and quite forget what thou amongst the leaves has never known"' (p. 44). Between the acts of the pageant Isa does fade off:

> 'Where do I wander?' she mused. 'Down what draughty tunnels? Where the eyeless wind blows? . . . In some harvestless dim field where no evening lets fall her mantle; nor sun rises. All's equal there. Unblowing, ungrowing are the roses there. Change is not; nor the mutable and lovable; nor greetings nor partings; nor furtive findings and feelings, where hand seeks hand and eye seeks shelter from the eye.'   (p. 113)

The description recalls Mrs Ramsay's 'strange no man's land', but Isa enjoys none of the ecstasy usually associated with such experience. Only little George is granted a moment of being:

> George grubbed. The flower blazed between the angles of the roots. . . . All that inner darkness became a hall, leaf smelling, earth smelling of yellow light. And the tree was beyond the flower; the grass, the flower and the tree were entire. Down on his knees grubbing he held the flower complete.   (pp. 12–13)

But this too is quickly shattered by something terrifying and eyeless, 'a terrible peaked eyeless monster, moving on legs, brandishing arms' – Mr Oliver in a paper hat.

The central action of this novel is not a perceptual event, the apprehension of pure being by a sensitive central character, like Rachel, or Mrs Ramsay; it is the physical action of Giles Oliver, who encounters a snake choking with a toad in its mouth:

> The snake was unable to swallow; the toad was unable to die. A spasm made the ribs contract; blood oozed. It was birth the wrong way round – a monstrous inversion. So, raising his foot, he stamped on them. The mass crushed and slithered. The white canvas on his tennis shoes was bloodstained and sticky. But it was action.   (p. 75)

The text does not particularly endorse this action, but neither does it condemn it. In *To the Lighthouse* Lily speaks of 'the ineffectiveness of action, the supremacy of thought' (*TL*, 181). Here there is no creative counterpoint to Giles's action: Isa's vision is a negative one, La Trobe's pageant gets stuck on 'un/dis'. Thought, and the transforming power of the imagination, are no longer supreme. We are, at the end, poised between unity and dispersity, between fragmentation and wholeness. In her other novels Woolf had explored the tension between various contraries, but now, unlike in *To the Lighthouse*, the work of art (either that within the narrative or the text itself) offers no means of transcending that opposition.

There are obvious symbolic and mythic elements in the text, but these too fail to provide order. Isa is thirty-nine years old, 'the age of the century', and she has been coming to the pageant for the proverbial seven years, seven times repeating the discussion about how it will be 'wet or fine' (p. 20). The Barn reminds the visitors of a Greek temple, or of the Middle Ages, or at least of some age before their own (pp. 23, 75–6). But neither the pageant nor the manor house create community. The Barn reminds people of Greece, but it evokes nothing of the 'Greek Spirit' that seemed so important in *Jacob's Room*.

Nothing coheres. It is a condition captured by the phrase 'orts, scraps and fragments', a phrase often used in describing the form of the book. I would argue that the phrase provides much more than just a convenient description of the disconnected quality of *Between the Acts*. It appears five times, from four different speakers, in the last twenty pages of the novel. It issues first from behind a bush as 'a megaphontic, anonymous, loud-speaking affirmation' (my italics throughout):

> Look at ourselves, ladies and gentlemen! Then at the wall: and ask how's this wall, the great wall, which we call, perhaps miscall, civilization, to be built by (here the mirrors flicked and flashed) *orts, scraps and fragments* like outselves?   (p. 136)

And it appears again at the close of the same speech, in connection with the human values that constitute civilisation:

> note too in to-day's paper 'Dearly loved by his wife'; and the impulse which leads us – mark you, when no one's looking – to the window at midnight to smell the bean.... There is such a thing – you can't deny it. What? You can't descry it? All you can see of yourselves is *scraps, orts and fragments*?   (p. 136)

Then the narrator picks it up, asking hesitantly,

> Was that voice ourselves? *Scraps, orts and fragments*, are we, also, that?   (p. 137)

Next, Reverend Streatfield incorporates it in his summation:

> 'I caught myself too reflected, as it happened in my own mirror ...' (Laughter) '*Scraps, orts and fragments*! Surely we should unite?'   (p. 140, Woolf's ellipsis)

Finally Isa, pondering what the Reverend has said, that 'We act different parts but are the same', muses:

'*Orts, scraps and fragments,*' she quoted what she remembered of the vanishing play. (p. 156)

Significantly, only the first and the last passages appear in the first typescript of the novel.[4] Woolf felt the phrase was important enough to add three more instances of it in the second typescript, and to add two anticipatory references to 'scraps and fragments' earlier in the book:

> *Scraps and fragments* reached Miss La Trobe where she stood, script in hand, behind the tree. (p. 90)

> Every moment the audience slipped the noose; split up into *scraps and fragments.* (p. 90)

The phrase thus emphasises the fragmentation of civilisation, of human character, of the pageant, and, by extension, of the text itself.

However, the phrase is not Woolf's own. It comes from *Troilus and Cressida*, iv, ii, spoken by Troilus at the end of his speech to Ulysses as he watched in anguished disbelief as Cressida flirts with Diomed:

> This she? no, this is Diomed's Cressida.
> If beauty have a soul, this is not she;
>   · · ·
>   O madness of discourse,
> That cause sets up with and against itself;
> Bi-fold authority, where reason can revolt
> Without perdition, and loss assume all reason
> Without revolt. This is, and is not, Cressid.
>   · · ·
> Instance, O instance, strong as Pluto's gates;
> Cressid is mine, tied with the bonds of heaven.
> Instance, O instance, strong as heaven itself;
> The bonds of heaven are slipped, dissolved, and loosed;
> And with another knot, five-finger-tied,
> The fractions of her faith, orts of her love,
> The fragments, scraps, the bits, and greasy relics
> Of her o-er-eaten faith, are bound to Diomed.[5]

What needs to be said first is that the phrase is, then, not simply an expression of fragmentation in Woolf's novel, for while it does express fragmentation, it does at the same time establish a link with the literary tradition. But it is a link that questions itself in the process of making a connection, for it suggests that orts, after-dinner leavings, are all that we have left of Shakespeare. Everyone in *Between the Acts* misquotes, and when Bartholomew claims that the British are insensitive to painting, 'whereas, Mrs Manresa, if she'll allow me my old man's liberty, has her Shakespeare by heart', the lady can quote no further than the first line of Shakespeare's most famous soliloquy, 'To be or not to be'. Isa supplies some apposite lines on obliteration – 'Fade far away and quite forget what thou amongst the leaves hast never known' – which are, however, from Keats's *Ode to a Nightingale*; Dodge adds the next phrase from Keats's poem, 'The weariness, the torture, and the fret', and Shakespeare is lost. Bartholomew, none the less, is triumphant: 'There! ... That proves it!' (p. 44). Proves that the great unifying text of English literature has disintegrated.

But the implications of the phrase are still more complex. The allusion is to a play which is often considered to be Shakespeare's most modern play; one writer cites it in a list of 'postmodernist' works.[6] It is a play in which the characters are presented as the types they have come to be in memory: false Cressid, faithful Troilus, Pandarus – names which even by the time the play was written had become words in the language. They were already citations from another text. *Troilus and Cressida* foregrounds the inevitable element of citation in any writing – just as *Between the Acts* does. Thus the phrase does not function in the manner that, say, the allusion to Cymbeline ('fear no more the heat of the sun') does in *Mrs Dalloway*, as a personal touchstone for an individual charac-ter. It emphasises the extent to which all literature is citation, all the stories have already been told.[7]

What seems different in this novel is the attitude toward the fragmentation. There doesn't seem to be the same desperate need to create unity in the face of chaos (and the chaos is certainly not reduced) that there was in, say, *To the Lighthouse*. In fact, the novel exhibits many of the characteristics of that much-debated term, 'postmodernism'.[8] In the remarks that follow I necessarily over-simplify, but I am not trying to put *Between the Acts* into a postmodernist pigeon-hole, merely using a few of the less conten-

tious characteristics of postmodernism to help define the difference between Woolf's last novel and her earlier ones. To consider
tone first of all, the postmodernists see experience as random and
contingent, but they accept this; it is not a source of anxiety as it was
for the modernists. Denis Donoghue describes postmodernism as
'debonair' rather than 'doom-laden', content to let discrepancies
bloom rather than to search for unity.[9] This is consistent with the
bleakness and comedy critics have found in the book: the bleakness
is there all right, but it it not viewed with the same anxiety.

For modernists it is *self* which gives the world its meaning and
value. One's true life is lived within, and this leads to a quest for
revelation that transcends time and history: Proust's memories,
Joyce's epiphanies, Woolf's moments of being. With postmodernism the self is no longer regarded as something autonomous, which
then creates language and through it orders the world; the self is,
rather, something determined by language. The opening pages of
the novel are confusing because of the difficulty in establishing who
these characters are. Isa is abruptly referred to as 'Mrs Giles Oliver'
(p. 9); we've heard of her husband 'the stockbroker' but we don't
know his name, and the 'Mr Oliver' who is present is an old man
retired from the Indian Civil Service. Some readers have suggested
the confusion is the result of the novel being unrevised at Woolf's
death, but she had preserved the confusion through two typescript
drafts. A few pages later, Isa feels '"In love"' with the gentleman
farmer, and tests this phrase against her feeling for her husband,
'"The father of my children," she added, slipping into the cliché
conveniently provided by fiction' (p. 14). Woolf seems to be
exploring the way in which character, both in and out of the
pageant, is created by language, the codes and clichés of society. In
the 'orts and fragments' speech Troilus is also raising the question
of the stability of Cressida's selfhood, something she herself had
warned him about earlier: 'I have a kind of self resides with
you, / But an unkind self, that itself will leave / To be another's fool'
(III. ii. 144–8).

Woolf's previous work tended to privilege the world of art over
that of ordinary life.[10] For the postmodernists, on the other hand,
meaning is not to be found by transcending the world but by
involvement in it, and Alan Wilde argues persuasively that Woolf's
fiction moves away from the need to order and transcend the world
to a recognition of the phenomenal world, whatever its gaps and
fragments, as the source of experience.[11] Miss La Trobe's vision of

a new play comes to her in a smokey pub that stinks of stale beer, not in the blessed solitude Bernard had sought, and the words of one syllable that she too seeks bubble up from the mud. It is as if the street-singers of *Jacob's Room* and *Mrs Dalloway* are now united with the artist:

> Words of one syllable sank down into the mud. She drowsed; she nodded. The mud became fertile. Words rose above the intolerably laden dumb oxen plodding through the mud. Words without meaning – wonderful words.   (p. 153)

Further, the novel ends, not with the vision of the artist, nor with the central character encountering death, but with the primal struggle between man and woman, a struggle that will lead not to transcendent vision but to a physical, human birth:

> Alone, enmity was bared; also love. Before they slept, they must fight; after they had fought, they would embrace. From that embrace another life might be born. But first they must fight, as the dog fox fights with the vixen, in the heart of darkness, in the fields of night.   (p. 158)

The novel is grounded in social reality, and where modernism tended to be élitist about art, postmodernism blurs the boundary between high and low art, and the artistic production depicted in *Between the Acts* is not, for instance, a carefully wrought post-Impressionist painting as in *To the Lighthouse* (inaccessible to Mr Bankes or Mr Ramsay) but a highly amateur communal pageant. The characters, the country folk, and La Trobe's words are rooted in the earth.

In addition, the text is one of surfaces. There is no revelation, no meaning to be found in a transcendent symbol. In *Between the Acts* there is no lighthouse, not even a fin in a waste of waters, only the vase in the dining-room. The text is no longer a mirror of nature, as it was for the realists, or of the process of perception, as it was for the modernists; now the text only mirrors itself, playing with the notion of infinite mirroring regression. The mirrors at the end of the pageant mock the practice of mimetic fiction as well as the audience – and that audience is of course the reader as well as the characters in the novel. Part of this regressive mirroring takes the form of intertextual reference. Texts become part of all other texts, and history comes to be regarded as just one discourse among many. History implies the existence of a master narrative, a narrative which realistic fictions presented themselves as variations of, modernist fictions attempted to subvert (with their thrust toward the transcendental individual experience, a withdrawal from the world and time into the timeless world of art), and postmodernist texts render as intertextual collage, declining to fulfill causal expectations.[12] The pageant of *Between the Acts* has occasioned as much debate among the critics outside the book as among the audience within. What does it add up to? Is there a teleology? Woolf declines to answer, but it is clear that the pageant is nostalgic, like Troilus's cry a lament for what is past, for what perhaps never was.

Finally, the particular speech Wolf borrows from is famous for the problems it raises about language. The cry, 'O madness of discourse, / That cause sets up with and against itself' (III. ii. 139–40), has been much commented upon: is Troilus saying that discourse has momentarily gone mad, or that discourse is itself madness? Troilus is expressing the kind of rhetorical doubt that Puttenham called 'Aporia or the Doubtfull'. The term has gained a certain fame in our own time from the writings of Derrida, who uses it in the sense of a self-engendered paradox, but those implications exist in the term from the beginning for it derives from the Greek word meaning 'unpassable path'. This is the path that Woolf gives us. Truth is not to be found in a symbol but in the restless self-critique which endlessly defers the sense of an achieved self-identity, whether in the ideal of a language of full presence or the experience of a moment of being.

The movement is not toward transcendence but a return to the constant collision of contraries: the enmity of man and woman in the human realm, the 'madness of discourse' in the rhetorical realm. There is no 'pure' language. In *Jacob's Room* the narrator lamented that,

> Words have been used too often; touched and turned, and left exposed to the dust of the street. The words we seek hang close to the tree. We come at dawn and find them sweet beneath the leaf. (p. 90)

The language she now seeks is dusty but vital. Meaning is no longer to be found 'on the far side of language'; it is to be found down in the street. Her last essay, 'Anon', is an introduction to a new critical book on the history of English literature, a work she had been reading for all through the autumn of 1940 (conceived, significantly, while blackberrying, 12 September), and which she began writing promptly the day after she finished the first draft of *Between the Acts* (24 November 1940). In 'Anon' she speaks wistfully of the age before Caxton's printing press, when literature was communal and in flux. In a passage that recalls the mirrors of her novel, she says that in Malory's tales of Arthur,

> save that self consciousness had not yet raised its mirror, the men and women are ourselves, seen out of perspective; elongated, foreshortened, but very old, with a knowledge of all good and all evil. They are already corrupt in this fresh world. They have evil dreams. Arthur is doomed; the Queens are lustful. There never was, it seems, a time when men and women were without memory; There never was a young world.[13]

The same is true of language. There is always a trace. There never was a young word.

However, Woolf celebrates this: 'Behind the English lay ages of toil and love. That is the world beneath our consciousness; the anonymous world to which [in Malory] we can still return. . . . The voice is still the voice of Anon.' She laments that 'Caxton's printing press foretold the end of that anonymous world; It is now written down; fixed; nothing will be added' ('Anon', 385). But something of the free play of Anon was preserved by the early Elizabethan dramatists:

> Anonymity was a great possession. It gave the early writing an impersonality, a generality. . . . Anon the lyric poet repeats over and over again that flowers fade; that death is the end. He is never tired of celebrating red roses and white breasts. The anonymous playwright has like the singer this nameless vitality, something drawn from the crowd in the penny seats and not yet dead in ourselves.   ('Anon', 397–8)

Through Miss La Trobe (who has no first name and is referred to as 'Whatsername') and her pageant, Woolf seeks some of the 'nameless vitality' of Anon. She knows that she will never achieve the artlessness, the unselfconsciousness, of the early writers, but like them she celebrates the heterogeneity of life. She is no longer seeking to impose a unity. Like Shakespeare in *Troilus in Cressida*, Woolf is looking backward to create something new.

Thus *Between the Acts* is not Woolf's last confused or despairing cry before she walked into the river, and if the book seems at times a collection of scraps and fragments it is deliberately so, not a result of her not having completed the final revisions. It has been suggested that had Woolf lived she would have revised so as 'to align for greater consistency her levels of metaphor' and to achieve 'greater unity among the allusive fragments somewhat evenly dispersed throughout the novel's thirty seven scenes'.[14] Consistency was not her object. Woolf was testing the boundaries of language, as she had throughout her career, exploring here the complex web of relation between literature, history and common speech. *Between the Acts* testifies to her still vital creativity, to the fact that she was still in the vanguard of literary experiment, helping to create what would come to be defined as postmodernism, just as she had played such a central role in what has been called modernism.

In the last months of her life she continued *Reading at Random*, now called *Turning the Page*, with an essay called 'The Reader', which explores the historical development of the reader. She locates his emergence in the mid-seventeenth century, with Robert Burton's *The Anatomy of Melancholy*: 'It is here that we develop faculties that the play left dormant. Now the reader is completely in being.' Once again she defines the written text in terms of its movement away from the play. But where in 'Anon' she had concluded with the *end* of the freedom of the anonymous poet ('The playwright is replaced by the man who writes a book. The audience is replaced by the reader. Anon is dead'), in the fragments of this last essay she concludes with the *beginning* of freedom for the reader. She had said that 'The first blow has been aimed at Anon when the authors name is attached to the book' ('Anon', 385), but now that author/ity proves not to be a limiting factor, subverted as it is by the relation of the reader to the text, and the nature of the text itself:

> [The reader] can pause; he can ponder; he can compare; he can draw back from the page and see behind it a man sitting alone in the centre of the labyrinth of words in a college room thinking of suicide. He can gratify many different moods. He can read

directly what is on the page, or, drawing aside, can read what is not written. . . . We are in a world where nothing is concluded.   ('Reader', 429)

The image of the writer in the labyrinth of language recalls the Greeks and anticipates Borges, and the notion of a text that is never closed prefigures contemporary theories of reading. More to the point, however, though the reference to suicide inevitably makes us think of her own death, Woolf's words direct us not to the life but back to her own texts, and there, truly, 'we are in a world where nothing is concluded'.

Notes

Chapter 1 The Writer's Life

1. See S. P. Rosenbaum (ed.), *The Bloomsbury Group: A Collection of Memoirs, Commentary and Criticism* (Toronto: University of Toronto Press, 1975).
2. George, Gerald and Stella Duckworth were the children of Julia Stephen's first marriage. For an account of Woolf's relations with the Duckworth brothers see Louise DeSalvo, *Virginia Woolf: The Impact of Child Sexual Abuse on Her Life and Work* (Boston, Mass.: Beacon Press, 1989).
3. On the Hogarth Press see Leonard's biographies as well as J. Howard Woolmer, *A Checklist of the Hogarth Press, 1917–1946*, with a short history of the press by Mary E. Gaither (Revere, Penn.: Woolmer/ Brotherston, 1986); Donna E. Rheim, *The Handprinted Books of Leonard and Virginia Woolf at the Hogarth Press, 1917–1932* (Ann Arbor, Mich.: UMI Research Press, 1985); John Lehmann, *Thrown to the Woolfs: Leonard and Virginia Woolf and the Hogarth Press* (New York: Holt, Rinehart and Winston, 1979); Richard Kennedy, *A Boy at the Hogarth Press* (New York: Heinemann, 1972).
4. *The Letters of Vita Sackville-West to Virginia Woolf*, ed. Louise DeSalvo and Mitchell Leaska (New York: William Morrow, 1985).
5. For an account of the novel's development see Mitchell Leaska's introduction to his edition of *'The Pargiters': The Novel-Essay Portion of 'The Years'* (London: Hogarth Press, 1978), and Grace Radin's *Virginia Woolf's 'The Years': The Evolution of a Novel* (Knoxville, Tenn.: University of Tennessee Press, 1981).

Chapter 2 *The Voyage Out*

1. In 'A Sketch of the Past', in her account of reading a poem and suddenly having it become 'altogether intelligible', an experience that was probably the original for Rachel's (quoted above, p. 16), Woolf indicates that an intimate relation exists among moments of being, the process by which they are realised in language, and the kind of reading in which words become 'experienced'.

   Ernst Cassirer, exploring the creation of language in his *Language and Myth*, trans. Susan K. Langer (New York: Dover, 1953), deals with transactions strikingly similar to those Rachel participates in (see pp. 23, 36, 58).

2. Louise A. DeSalvo (ed.), *'Melymbrosia' by Virginia Woolf: An Early Version of The Voyage Out'* (New York: New York Public Library, 1982) p. 132.

3. These two passages (pp. 222, 223–4) were deleted in the American edition, but not because Woolf no longer endorsed Terence's comments. Louise A. DeSalvo observes that, as opposed to the British edition, in the American edition Rachel and Terence say very little to each other, and even the conversations they do have are summarised, not presented directly. DeSalvo suggests that Woolf was deliberately moving closer to the vagueness and universality that E. M. Forster had remarked in the 1915 edition, and closer to Terence's proposed novel about Silence. See *Virginia Woolf's First Voyage: A Novel in the Making* (London: Macmillan, 1980) p. 114.

More generally, DeSalvo argues that in the passage from *Melymbrosia* to *The Voyage Out* Woolf, in an act of self-censorship, moved away from the bluntness and candour of the earlier version, as her flirtation with Clive Bell gradually resolved into something less intense (*First Voyage*, pp. 63–6) pointing out that the earlier draft 'bristles with social commentary' (*Melymbrosia*, p. xxxvi).

Jane Marcus argues categorically that 'in the case of Virginia Woolf, very often the drafts and unpublished versions seemed "truer" texts. . . . The censorship of editors, publishers, husbands, as well as the enormous pressure of self-censorship on a woman writer, makes the reader mistrust the published text and makes the critic mistrust any methodology that accepts without question the privilege of the printed text'; see *Virginia Woolf and the Languages of Patriarchy* (Bloomington, Ind.: Indiana University Press, 1987) p. xii.

In *The Voyage Out* the concern with social issues and the position of women is more explicit, but without denying the importance of Woolf's relationship with Clive Bell and her insecurities over publishing her first novel it is important to note that this same pattern obtained throughout her career, even after she became her own publisher. In the transition from draft to published text her art always became less overtly political.

4. In *The Voyage Out* there is already a dramatising of the connection made explicit in *A Room of One's Own* and *Three Guineas*: that artistic independence rests upon economic independence. Terence is in many ways the opposite of Richard Dalloway, but there is a clear link between the cultural imperialism of the one and the equally well-meaning domestic domination of the other. Terence is a sensitive man, but he still assumes power: 'I'd keep you free', he thinks to himself in the first flush of infatuation (p. 298), but will later tell her to answer their letters while he works on his novel: '"We're wasting the morning – I ought to be writing my book, and you ought to be answering these"' (p. 363).

5. She obviously found the phrase expressive. It recurs in the passage from 'On Not Knowing Greek' quoted above, and she uses it again in 1940 in her diary as she ponders the difficulties of literary criticism: 'I wish I could invent a new critical method – something swifter and

lighter and more colloquial and yet intense: more to the point and less composed; more fluid and following the flight than my C. R. essays. The old problem: how to keep the flight of the mind, yet be exact' (*D* v, 298).

Chapter 3 'Kew Gardens' and *Jacob's Room*

1. Her success in the piece was immediately recognised. Harold Child, writing in *The Times Literary Supplement* on the first appearance of 'Kew Gardens' (1919) lauded this 'new proof of the complete unimportance in art of the *hyle*, the subject matter':

> Titian paints Bacchus and Ariadne; and Rembrandt paints a hideous old woman.... And Mrs Woolf writes about Kew Gardens and a snail and some stupid people. But here is 'Kew Gardens' – a work of art, made, 'created', as we say, finished, four-square; a thing of original and therefore strange beauty, with its own 'atmosphere', its own vital force.

'Kew Gardens', unsigned review, *The Times Literary Supplement*, 29 May 1919, p. 293; reprinted in *Virginia Woolf: The Critical Heritage*, ed. Robin Majumdar and Allen McLaurin (London: Routledge & Kegan Paul, 1975) p. 67.
2. For a discussion of further permutations of 'it' see Avrom Fleishman, 'Forms of the Woolfian Short Story', in *Virginia Woolf: Revaluation and Continuity*, ed. Ralph Freedman (Berkeley, Cal.: University of California Press, 1980) pp. 54–5, on 'Solid Objects' and 'The New Dress'.
3. The holograph draft of the novel is contained in three volumes, housed in the Berg collection of the New York Public Library.

   In his pioneering study of Woolf, David Daiches concluded that the novel was written 'for the sake of the impressions, of the fluid rendering of experience – one might say, for the sake of style'; see *Virginia Woolf* (Norfolk, Va.: New Directions, 1942) p. 61.

   Sara Ruddick, on the other hand, argues for the centrality of social forces in the shaping of the novel, pointing out that although Jacob is modelled on Thoby Stephen, Jacob's death, unlike Thoby's, is not accidental: it is the 'avoidable outcome of institutionalized violence'; see 'Private Brother, Public World', in *New Feminist Essays on Virginia Woolf*, ed. Jane Marcus (London: Macmillan 1981) p. 193.
4. Woolf's own devotion to Greece is amply documented in her diary and in the essays 'The Perfect Language' (1927) and 'On Not Knowing Greek' (1925). The notion of a 'common mind' appears as early as 1903, when Woolf was 21: 'I think I see for a moment how our minds are all threaded together – how any live mind today is ⟨conne⟩ of the very same stuff as Plato's & Euripides. It is only a continuation & development of the same thing – It is this common mind that binds the whole world together; & all the world is mind'. Quoted by Brenda Silver in her introduction to *Virginia Woolf's Reading Notebooks* (Princeton, N.J.: Princeton University Press, 1983) p. 5.

5. Judy Little contends that the book is actually an 'attack' on the form: 'It seems almost as though Virginia Woolf deliberately chose the traditions of the *Bildungsroman* in order to play havoc with them'; see '*Jacob's Room* as Comedy: Virginia Woolf's Parodic *Bildungsroman*', in Marcus (ed.), *New Feminist Essays*, p. 109. Zwerdling notes that 'unlike the conventional *Bildungsroman*, *Jacob's Room* lacks a teleology' (*Virginia Woolf and the Real World* (Berkeley, Cal.: University of California Press, 1986) p. 898); and Avrom Fleishman argues that Woolf's novel extends the form into 'a fitful sequence of unachieved experiences rather than a coherent process'; see *Virginia Woolf: A Critical Reading* (Baltimore, Md.: Johns Hopkins Press, 1975) p. 46. See also Ralph Freedman, 'The Form of Fact and Fiction: Jacob's Room as Paradigm', in Freedman (ed.), *Virginia Woolf*, pp. 129–31.

   Early commentators, such as James Hafley in *The Glass Roof: Virginia Woolf as Novelist* (Berkeley, Cal.: University of California Press, 1954) pp. 58–9, and J. K. Johnstone in *The Bloomsbury Group: A Study of E. M. Forster, Lytton Strachey, Virginia Woolf, and Their Circle* (London: Secker & Warburg, 1954) p. 328, criticised the form, but recent critics have found it appropriate, and have been more concerned with the shifts in narrative point of view. Virginia Blain argues that 'Woolf's technique deconstructs the whole notion of an integrated self as a unifying principle either for characterization or narration'; see 'Narrative Voice and the Female Perspective in Virginia Woolf's Early Novels', in *Virginia Woolf: New Critical Essays*, ed. Patricia Clements and Isobel Grundy (London: Vision Press, 1983) p. 133.

Chapter 4 *Mrs Dalloway*

1. See, for example, Stefan Oltean, 'Textual Functions of Free Indirect Discourse in the Novel *Mrs Dalloway* by Virginia Woolf', *Revue romaine de linguistique*, no. 26 (November–December 1981) 533–47.
2. James Naremore, *The World Without a Self: Virginia Woolf and the Novel* (New Haven, Conn.: Yale University Press, 1973) pp. 87, 90. See also Susan Dick, 'The Tunnelling Process: Some Aspects of Virginia Woolf's Use of Memory and the Past', in *Virginia Woolf: New Critical Essays*, ed. Patricia Clements and Isobel Grundy (London: Vision Press, 1983) p. 189; J. Hillis Miller, *Fiction and Repetition: Seven English Novels* (Cambridge, Mass.: Harvard University Press, 1982) p. 178.
3. Miller, *Fiction and Repetition*, pp. 183–4.
4. The main body of the Dalloway manuscript is in three volumes in the British Library: Additional Manuscripts nos 51044, 51045, 51046 (those interested in consulting the manuscripts should be aware that vol. III is actually a long section that belongs in the middle of volume II, at MS. p. 109 with a scene that corresponds to p. 157 in the Hogarth edition). Preliminary notes and the opening sections are in the Berg Collection of the New York Public Library.
5. Beverley Ann Schlack, *Continuing Presences: Virginia Woolf's Use of Literary Allusion* (University Park, Penn.: Pennsylvania State University

Press, 1979) p. 63. Also see Schlack on the connection between Septimus and the circle of the Sodomites – the seventh/Septimus circle – in Dante's *Inferno* (ibid., pp. 68–72).

6. Walter J. Ong, offering the analogy of a bass viol which will vibrate in sympathy when another is strummed nearby, argues that sound unites groups of living things as nothing else can. It is these initial connections that form the basis of the party. Ong insists that we should not think of the word as a record, that in fact its natural habitat is sound; writing distances one from actuality, thus 'by comparison with the oral medium, writing and print are permanently decadent' (p. 138).

   Jacques Derrida, of course, vigorously opposes such assumptions. He contends that origin or pure presence is an *ignis fatuus*, that there is a system of distinctions or differences that is prior to any utterance, and thus that writing, far from being the shadow of speech is (because it is the signifier of a signifier) the proper model for the way language works. Writing may be, as Ong says, inevitably decadent, but traces of this decadence are always already present in speech as well.

   These views, and the emphasis on language as a self-enclosed system capable of free play, would seem to be inimical to Woolf, who patently believes in a transcendental signified and in the ability of language to embody it. But Woolf's fictions enact a deep-seated ambivalence toward language. In *The Waves* Bernard says, 'I need a howl; a cry' (p. 199), a statement at odds with the highly formal, even iconic, text that contains it. Yet it is a text of voices.

   See Walter J. Ong, *The Presence of the Word: Some Prolegomena for Cultural and Religious History* (New Haven, Conn.: Yale University Press, 1967) p. 123; and Jacques Derrida, *Of Grammatology*, trans. Gayatri Spivak (Baltimore, Md.: Johns Hopkins University Press, 1976) pp. 35, 44.

7. On Woolf's conversation see QB ii, 144–6.

8. Maria DiBattista views the skywriting scene as 'Woolf's gentle satire on the symbolizing powers of the mind'; see 'Joyce, Woolf and the Modern Mind', in Clements and Grundy (eds), *Virginia Woolf: New Critical Essays*, p. 108.

9. Norman Page, *Speech in the English Novel* (London: Longman, 1973) p. 42.

10. In the manuscript the interview between Septimus and Bradshaw is a confrontation, with Septimus asserting, '"We will have this out, Sir William" . . . hunching himself up in his chair' (MS. no. 51044, p. 133), where in the final text he stammers helplessly, his responses unvoiced (pp. 106–9).

    The whole movement from manuscript to published text is one of greater indirection (as it is with most of the novels). For instance, when Clarissa meditates on why she gives her parties, Woolf ties the desire specifically to the artistic impulse: 'And she did it because it was an offering. Just as somebody writes a book after all' (MS. no. 51045, pp. 54–5). In the published version the connection is implied (pp. 134–5).

11. George Steiner, *Language and Silence: Essays on Language, Literature and the Inhuman* (New York: Atheneum, 1967) p. 27.

12. See Howard Harper, *Between Language and Silence: The Novels of Virginia Woolf* (Baton Rouge, La.: Louisiana State University Press, 1982) pp. 123, 133; Miller, *Fiction and Repetition*, p. 195; and Lucio Ruotolo, *Six Existential Heroes: The Politics of Faith* (Cambridge, Mass.: Harvard University Press, 1973) p. 35.
13. See, for example, Ted Cohen, 'Metaphor and the Cultivation of Intimacy', in *On Metaphor*, ed. Sheldon Sacks (Chicago, Ill.: Chicago University Press, 1978) p. 6, and Patricia Parker, 'The Metaphorical Plot', in *Metaphor: Problems and Perspectives*, ed. David S. Miall (Brighton: Harvester Press, 1982) pp. 133–57.
14. Ruotolo, *Six Existential Heroes*, p. 29.
15. Miller, *Fiction and Repetition*, 190.
16. Walter Benjamin, *The Origin of German Tragic Drama*, trans. John Osborne (London: NLB, 1977) p. 201.

Chapter 5   The Essays

1. Jane Novak, *The Razor Edge of Balance: A Study of Virginia Woolf* (Coral Gables, Fla.: University of Miami Press, 1975) p. 44.
2. The only book-length study of the essays, Mark Goldman's *The Reader's Art: Virginia Woolf as Literary Critic* (The Hague: Mouton, 1976) is devoted to tracing 'dominant themes that will reveal an underlying form or controlling aesthetic' (p. 3). Barbara Bell and Carol Ohmann provide a very good analysis of Woolf's method in their brief but incisive 'Virginia Woolf's Criticism: a Polemical Preface', *Critical Inquiry*, vol. 1 (1974) pp. 361–71. Elizabeth Pomeroy, in a more specialised essay, concludes that Woolf's essays 'refine the novelist's skills: characterization through detail, the pacing of a narrative, or the polishing of an image which casts light in different directions like a prism'; see 'Garden and Wilderness: Virginia Woolf Reads the Elizabethans', *Modern Fiction Studies*, vol. 24 (1978–9) p. 504.
3. Virginia Woolf, *Books and Portraits: Some Further Selections from her Literary and Biographical Writings*, ed. Mary Lyon (London: Hogarth Press, 1977) p. 33.
4. Thomas J. Farrell, 'The Female and Male Modes of Rhetoric', *College English*, 40 (1979) p. 915.
5. Christine Brooke-Rose, *A Grammar of Metaphor* (London: Secker & Warburg, 1958) p. 206.
6. Irma Rantavaara, *Virgina Woolf's 'The Waves'* (Port Washington, Wis.: Kennikat, 1969) p. 43.
7. Sir Paul Harvey (ed.), *The Oxford Companion to English Literature*, 4th edn (Oxford: Oxford University Press, 1967) p. 150. See Patricia Parker's discussion of metaphor as 'alien', 'boundary-crosser' or 'exile' in 'The Metaphorical Plot' in *Metaphor: Problems and Perspectives*, ed. David S. Miall (Brighton: Harvester Press) pp. 133–7.
8. Paul de Man, 'The Epistemology of Metaphor', in *On Metaphor*, ed. Sheldon Sacks (Chicago, Ill.: Chicago University Press, 1978) p. 19.
9. Paul Ricoeur, *The Rule of Metaphor: Multi-disciplinary Studies of the*

Creation of Meaning in Language, trans. Robert Czerny (Toronto: University of Toronto Press, 1977) pp. 39, 244–5.
10. Michael J. Reddy, 'The Conduit Metaphor – a Case of Frame Conflict in Our Language about Language', in *Metaphor and Thought*, ed. Andrew Ortony (Cambridge: Cambridge University Press, 1979) pp. 184–224.

Chapter 6   *To the Lighthouse*

1. The way we read that final line varies tremendously depending upon what edition we have before us. Mr Ramsay wants his wife to say that she loves him; she feels she cannot do it. The British edition reads,

> 'Yes, you were right. It's going to be wet to-morrow.' She had not said it, but he knew it. And she looked at him smiling. For she had triumphed again.

He knows, but she has triumphed; and the smile has something of a smirk. Yet for the American edition Woolf altered these lines and produced a very different effect:

> 'Yes, you were right. It's going to be wet to-morrow. You won't be able to go.' And she looked at him smiling. For she had triumphed again. She had not said it; he knew.

'You won't be able to go' is a fuller acknowledgement of Mr Ramsay's position than the admission that 'It's going to be wet tomorrow'. More important, the final statement is poised on the semicolon. Mrs Ramsay has not had to submit and declare her love, yet at the same time she has made her husband feel loved and Mr Ramsay has not demeaned himself by once more demanding love; both have retained their integrity and their dignity.
   J. A. Lavin points out that although the British and American editions were published simultaneously on 5 May 1927, the American edition was prepared from proofs made up by the Hogarth Press, proofs which Woolf altered. Because the editions were published at the same time, however, readers have just assumed that they are identical. See the 'First Editions of Virginia Woolf's *To the Lighthouse*' in *Proof: The Yearbook of American Bibliographical and Textual Studies*, ed. Joseph Katz, vol. 2 (Columbia, S.C.: University of South Carolina Press, 1972) pp. 185–211.
2. See Avrom Fleishman, *Virginia Woolf: A Critical Reading* (Baltimore, Md.: Johns Hopkins Press, 1975) pp. 117–18 for a discussion of the significance of the quoted and unquoted stanzas of this poem by Charles Elton.
3. P. 45, heightened in the American edition to '*his glory* in the phrases that he made' (p. 70, my italics).
4. Gayatri Spivak, 'Unmaking and Making in *To the Lighthouse*', in *Reading*

Women Writing, ed. Sally McConnell-Ginet, Ruth Borker and Nelly Furman (New York: Praeger, 1980) p. 321.

5. Reprinted in Michèle Barrett (ed.), *Virginia Woolf, Women and Writing* (Toronto: Quadrant Editions, 1979) pp. 184–5.

6. See Barrett, *Virginia Woolf,* p. 33; Sandra Gilbert, 'Woman's Sentence, Man's Sentencing: Linguistic Fantasies in Woolf and Joyce', in *Virginia Woolf and Bloomsbury: A Centenary Celebration,* ed. Jane Marcus (London: Macmillan, 1987) p. 209; Luce Irigaray, 'Ce sexe qui n'en est pas un', in *New French Feminisms,* ed. Elaine Marks and Isabelle de Courtivron (Amherst, Mass.: University of Massachusetts Press, 1980) p. 103; Jane Marcus, *Virgina Woolf and the Languages of Patriarchy* (Bloomington, Ind.: Indiana University Press, 1987) pp. 12–14, 37, 169.

7. The passage in *Room* describes both the syntax and the larger narrative strategy of *To the Lighthouse*:

> 'Then she had gone further and broken the sequence – the expected order.... the effect was somehow baffling; one could not see a wave heaping itself, a crisis coming round the next corner ... whenever I was about to feel the usual things in the usual places, about love, about death, the annoying creature twitched me away, as if the important point were just a little further on.   (p. 87)

Chapter 7   *The Waves*

1. As the first reviews appeared Woolf noted, 'Odd, that they [*The Times*] shd. praise my characters when I meant to have none' (*D* iv, 47).

2. In this paragraph and the next I am particularly indebted to John Graham's 'Point of View in *The Waves*: Some Services of the Style', *University of Toronto Quarterly,* vol. 29, no. 3 (April 1970) pp. 193–211, an article that remains indispensable to any commentary on *The Waves*'.

3. Pamela Transue, *Virginia Woolf and the Politics of Style* (Albany, N.Y.: State University of New York Press, 1986) p. 138.

4. Milan Kundera, *The Art of the Novel* (New York: Harper & Row, 1988) p. 148.

5. David Dowling, in *Bloomsbury Aesthetics and the Novels of Forster and Woolf* (London: Macmillan, 1985), sees a correspondence between *The Waves* and Beethoven's C minor quartet, with its 'grim tragic theme' in the final movement (p. 188). Gerald Levin, in 'The Musical Structure of *The Waves*', *Journal of Narrative Technique,* vol. 13, no. 3 (Fall 1983), suggests Woolf may have been influenced not only by listening to the quartets but by reading J. W. N. Sullivan's 1927 book on them. Levin observes that Sullivan's characterisation of the Opus 130 Fugue as a 'reconciliation of freedom and necessity, or of assertion and submission' suggests the major theme of Bernard's summation (p. 166).

6. Fleishman, *Virginia Woolf,* p. 155. See also Dowling, *Bloomsbury Aesthetics,* pp. 173–4, and John Graham, 'Manuscript Revision and the Heroic Theme of *The Waves*', *Twentieth Century Literature,* vol. 29, no. 3

(Fall 1983) pp. 328–9, where he states that over the course of Draft II Woolf made the interludes fewer and longer, playing down the parallels between them and the episodes and giving them a more uniform structure so that the reader would be reminded of the previous interlude as he or she read each new one.

7. Fleishman identifies seven different theories in his development (*Virginia Woolf*, pp. 164–6).

8. In his introduction to '*The Waves': The Two Holograph Drafts* (Toronto: University of Toronto Press, 1976), John Graham notes that the vision 'not only provided the experience out of which *The Waves* grew but also remained for Virginia Woolf a constant goal and measure of the entire creative process involved in writing it'. Further, he points out that 'the vision is implicit in the various plans and sketches drawn up between the time she recorded it and the time, three years later, when she began to write the first draft' (p. 16).

9. Graham, 'Point of View', p. 207.

10. T. S. Eliot, *Collected Poems* (London: Faber & Faber, 1975) p. 194, ll. 139–43.

Chapter 8 *Between the Acts*

1. Jean Guiguet found it bitter and bleak; see *Virginia Woolf and Her Works*, trans. Jean Stewart (London: Hogarth Press, 1965) p, 326. But Joan Bennett stressed the element of social comedy and saw in the pageant an affirmation of cultural community; see *Virginia Woolf: Her Art as a Novelist* (London: Cambridge University Press, 1964) p. 131.

In a later generation of critics writers such as Jean Wyatt and Alex Zwerdling maintain that only the dimmer characters, like the Rev. Streatfield, think of the pageant as affirmative, and that what the pageant actually does is to draw the spectators together only to finally expose the notion of a shared cultural heritage as an illusion; see Wyatt's 'Art and Allusion in *Between the Acts'*, *Mosaic*, vol. 11, no. 4 (Summer 1978) 96; and Zwerdling's *Virginia Woolf and the Real World* (Berkeley, Cal.: University of California Press, 1986) p. 321.

If the pageant is not positive, at least the animating force of nature is, claims Harriet Blodgett; it affirms life's vital potential; see 'The Nature of *Between the Acts'*, *Modern Language Studies*, vol. 13, no. 3 (1983) pp. 27–37.

Not so, declares L. J. Swingle, who argues persuasively that Woolf had been, throughout her career, committed to the Romantic ideal of gaining freedom through creativity, but that with *Between the Acts* she had come to regard creativity not as a divine spark but as a mere instinctual impulse, an extension of the sexual. Thus the only thing that can free man from nature is destruction (expressed in Giles's crushing of the snake and toad) – a belief so intolerable that the only course in her personal life was suicide; see 'Virginia Woolf and Romantic Prometheanism', *Bucknell Review*, vol. 25, no. 2 (1980) pp. 88–105.

And indeed the editor of the typescript, Mitchell Leaska, calls the novel the 'longest suicide note in the language. Certainly ... the most exquisitely written'; see his afterword to *Pointz Hall: The Early and Later Typescripts of* 'Between the Acts' (New York: John Jay Press, 1983) p. 451.

Yet Susan Kenney, in a sensitive analysis of the typescript drafts, contends that in the book 'the life instinct triumphs over chaos' and that Woolf's suicide was a smaller triumph, preserving her control over the integrity of her self; 'Two Endings: Virginia Woolf's Suicide and *Between the Acts*', *University of Toronto Quarterly*, vol. 44, no. 4 (Summer 1975) pp. 265–89.

Even in assessing the form of the book readers disagree, Naremore seeing in it tentative efforts to find a new kind of language (*The World Without a Self: Virginia Woolf and the Novel* (New Haven, Conn.: Yale University Press, 1973) (p. 246), S. P. Rosenbaum maintaining it is closer to *The Voyage Out* and *Night and Day*; see 'The Philosophical Realism of Virginia Woolf' in *English Literature and British Philosophy*, ed. S. P. Rosenbaum (Chicago, Ill. and London: University of Chicago Press, 1971) p. 355. Alan Wilde claims that, far from being a regression to a more traditional mode, it is in the vanguard of postmodernism; see 'Touching Earth: Virginia Woolf and the Prose of the World', in William E. Cain (ed.), *Philosophical Approaches to Literature: New Essays on Nineteenth and Twentieth Century Texts* (Lewisburg, Pa.: Bucknell University Press, 1984) pp. 140–64.

2. Swingle, 'Virginia Woolf and Romantic Prometheanism', p. 96.
3. See Naremore, *The World Without a Self*, p. 228.
4. See Leaska, *Pointz Hall*, 'Early Typescript', pp. 163 and 182, 'Later Typescript', pp. 353, 354, 409, 410, 412, 435.
5. *Troilus and Cressida* in *William Shakespeare: The Complete Works* (Baltimore, Md.: Penguin, 1969), IV. ii. 133–56. Woolf was very much aware of the play. Jeanne T. Newlin discusses the major British productions of the play in this century, one of which in particular probably influenced Woolf, the 21 September 1938 production, done in modern dress. It was staged as an anti-war play, which was certainly topical: Chamberlain had flown to Bad Godesberg the week before, and a week after the play's opening he signed the Munich Pact giving Hitler the Sudetenland. Woolf's friend Desmond McCarthy praised the production in the *New Statesman and Nation* for 1 October 1938, and later that week Woolf read and made notes on the play. Newlin observes that since the eighteenth century the play has been called the most 'modern' of Shakespeare's plays; see 'The Modernity of *Troilus and Cressida*: the case for Theatrical Criticism', *Harvard Library Bulletin*, vol. 27, no. 4 (October 1969) pp. 353–73.
6. William V. Spanos notes the postmodernity of Shakespeare's problem plays; see 'The Detective and the Boundary: Some Notes on the Postmodern Literary Imagination', *Boundary 2*, vol. 1, no. 1 (Fall 1972) p. 151.
7. See Elizabeth Freund, '"Ariachne's Broken Woof"': the Rhetoric of Citation in *Troilus and Cressida*', in Patricia Parker and Geoffrey

Hartman (eds), *Shakespeare and the Question of Theory: Language, Rhetoric, Deconstruction* (New York: Methuen, 1985) pp. 19–36.

8. Useful articles to start with in tracking the debate are the essays by John Barth, 'The Literature of Exhaustion' and 'The Literature of Replenishment: Postmodernist Fiction', *Atlantic Monthly*, vol. 220 (1967) pp. 29–34; and vol. 245 (1980) pp. 65–71; the articles by Ihab Hassan, Julia Kristeva and others in the *Bucknell Review*, vol. 25, no. 2 (1980), and the discussion in the *New Left Review*, vol. 146 (July–Aug. 1984) and subsequent issues, by Frederic Jameson, Perry Anderson and others. For a good overview see Linda Hutcheon's 30-page bibliography in *A Poetics of Postmodernism: History, Theory, Fiction* (London and New York: Routledge & Kegan Paul, 1988).

9. Denis Donoghue, 'The Promiscuous Cool of Postmodernism', *New York Times Book Review*, 22 Jane 1986, pp. 1, 36–9.

10. See David Lodge, *The Modes of Modern Writing* (London: Edward Arnold, 1977) pp. 220–45.

11. Wilde, 'Touching Earth', p. 161. I have also drawn on his discussion of Woolf and postmodernism in *Horizons of Assent: Modernism, Postmodernism, and the Ironic Imagination* (Baltimore, Md.: Johns Hopkins University Press, 1981).

12. See Allen Thiher, *Words in Reflection: Modern Language Theory and Postmodern Fiction* (Chicago, Ill.: University of Chicago Press, 1984) p. 188. Here and elsewhere in this chapter I am indebted to Thiher's lucid study of postmodernism.

13. '"Anon" and "The Reader": Virginia Woolf's Last Essays', ed. with intro. by Brenda R. Silver, *Twentieth Century Literature*, vol. 25 (Fall–Winter 1979) p. 385. See also Nora Eisenberg, 'Virginia Woolf's Last Word on Words: *Between the Acts* and "Anon"', in *New Feminist Essays on Virginia Woolf*, ed. Jane Marcus (London: Macmillan, 1981) pp. 253–66.

14. Leaska, *Pointz Hall*, p. xiv.

Select Bibliography

NOTES ON EDITIONS

The standard abbreviations for Virginia Woolf's works and the Quentin Bell biography have been used throughout. References to the novels are to the Granta editions; references to the *Diary, Letters* and memoirs are to the Hogarth Press editions; references to the essays are to the Hogarth four-volume *Collected Essays*, edited by Leonard Woolf.

NOVELS AND ESSAYS PUBLISHED DURING VIRGINIA WOOLF'S LIFETIME

The Voyage Out (VO), 1915
Night and Day, 1919
Jacob's Room (JR), 1922
The Common Reader, 1925
Mrs Dalloway (MD), 1925
To the Lighthouse (TL), 1927
Orlando, 1928
A Room of One's Own (Room), 1929
The Waves (W), 1931
Common Reader, 2nd ser., 1932
Flush, 1933
The Years, 1937
Three Guineas, 1938
Roger Fry, 1940
Between the Acts (BA), 1941

LETTERS, DIARIES, MEMOIRS

The Letters of Virginia Woolf (L), 6 vols, ed. Nigel Nicolson and Joanne Trautmann (1975–80).
The Diary of Virginia Woolf (D), 5 vols, ed. Anne Olivier Bell and Andrew McNeillie (1977–84).

Moments of Being: Unpublished Autobiographical Writings of Virginia Woolf (*MB*), 2nd edn, ed. Jeanne Schulkind (1985).

MANUSCRIPTS

DeSalvo, Louise A. (ed.), *'Melymbrosia' by Virginia Woolf: An Early Version of 'The Voyage Out'* (New York: New York Public Library, 1980).
Dick, Susan (ed.), *'To the Lighthouse': The Holograph Draft* (Toronto: University of Toronto Press, 1982).
Graham, J. W. (ed.), *'The Waves': The Two Holograph Drafts* (Toronto: University of Toronto Press, 1976).
Leaska, Mitchell A. (ed.), *'The Pargiters' by Virginia Woolf: The Novel-Essay Portion of 'The Years'* (London: Hogarth Press, 1978).
——, *'Pointz Hall': The Earlier and Later Typescripts of 'Between the Acts'* (New York: University Publications, 1983).

The principal manuscript collections in the United States are the Henry W. and Albert A. Berg Collection of English and American Literature of the New York Public Library, Astor, Lenox and Tilden Foundations, and, in Britain, The Monk's House Papers, University of Sussex, and the British Library.

BIBLIOGRAPHIES

Kirkpatrick, B. J., *A Bibliography of Virginia Woolf*, 3rd edn (Oxford: Clarendon Press, 1980).
Woolmer, J. Howard, *A Checklist of the Hogarth Press, 1917–1938*, with a short history of the press by Mary E. Gaither (New York: Woolmer/Brotherson, 1976).

BIOGRAPHIES

Bell, Quentin, *Virginia Woolf* (*QB*), (London: Hogarth Press, 1972).
Gordon, Lyndall, *A Writer's Life* (London: Oxford University Press, 1984).
Poole, Roger, *The Unknown Virginia Woolf* (Cambridge: Cambridge University Press, 1978).
Rose, Phyllis, *Woman of Letters: A Life of Virginia Woolf* (London: Routledge & Kegan Paul, 1978).
Spater, George, and Ian Parsons, *A Marriage of True Minds: An Intimate Portrait of Leonard and Virginia Woolf* (London: Jonathan Cape, 1977).
Trombley, Stephen, *'All that summer she was mad': Virginia Woolf and her Doctors* (London: Junction Books, 1981).

Index